Copyright 2023 ©

All rights reserved. No part of this publication may be reproduced or distributed in any form or by any means, electronic or mechanical, including photocopying, recording, or by any information storage or retrieval system, without the prior written consent of the author.

Front cover photo: Teresa Eileen Marie Christiansen

ISBN: 978-1-7775547-0-5

Riot is a first-time author living with her tiny dog, Leo, on Vancouver Island in beautiful British Columbia, Canada. As she was always attracted to words—reading by the age of three, dabbling in creative writing in university, and majoring in English Literature—it seemed inevitable that she would one day create something of her own to share with the masses.

Having undergone a traumatic ordeal in 2018, she began to use writing as a cathartic release: scratching out bits of her memories on recycled cash-out slips from her waitressing job. She compiled these slips, typed them out, and organized and reorganized them until things settled into a timeline that made sense. This is the book you hold in your hands, a completely raw and honest recollection of one year in Riot's journey with mental health.

She encourages you to share your own mental health stories at 'Shed the Shame' on Facebook in hopes of illuminating the truth that none of us suffer alone.

My journey affects your journey. We are all one world. And thus our stories unfold, united at their core, but oh so drastically different at the same time.

Be kind humans.

Hello, my name is Riot.

Or at least that's what my friends call me.

At this point I haven't done anything particularly riot-worthy in my life, and in fact spend most of my time following the rules and colouring inside the lines. I've always been a good girl.

But all that's about to change.

First, let's play a quick introduction game: three interesting things, one boring thing, and one thing you just didn't need to know about me. 1) I am a university graduate who got straight As in high school, made the Dean's List in university, and flat out walked away from a promising teaching career due to anxiety. 2) I love to play roller derby. If you've never heard of it, stop reading and Google immediately. This is where my name Riot originated. 3) I've lived and worked in Vietnam in a small city known for being one of the "seven new wonders of the world"[1]. One boring thing: I spend every morning watching Shark Tank or Dragon's Den to get my brain juices going. One thing you just didn't

---

[1] https://vietnamtourism.gov.vn/english/index.php/items/4566

need to know about me: I once pooped in a public pool...I was not an adult...I swear!

So now you know I'm all in. I've got no secrets. Why would I lie to you? This holds true for this entire collection of writing. Everything you read actually happened, and it happened without the influence of any hard drugs. This is a story about brain chemistry. I tell you this because the shit I'm about to claim seems nothing short of crazy. And drugs would be an easy explanation. But herein lies the point, my friends. We are far too quick to shun what we don't understand, to label and judge rather than to help, and to assume the worst of even those we know the best.

I lost many friends during this experience, I quit my roller derby league while on risk of suspension, and I left the man I'd loved for the past ten years of my life. Things were not right in my world. My brain was imbalanced.... but no one knew. And no one knew how to help.

In the following you'll meet a handful of people I consider influential in my journey; each one, whether big or small, good or bad, playing a role in my inevitable undoing.

I'd like to end.... or rather begin, by thanking you for

taking the time to walk this journey with me and meeting some of the characters who helped make me who I am today.

I am a strong believer that my journey affects your journey. We are all one world. And thus our stories unfold, united at their core, but oh so drastically different at the same time.

Be kind humans.

You know who's going through a lot right now?

Literally everyone.

Just be kind.

Even though an estimated 1 in 5 adults is experiencing mental illness at any given time, only about 40 percent seek treatment. Those who do seek treatment often wait a decade or more to get help."[2]

---

[2] https://www.inc.com/amy-morin/why-we-need-to-start-treating-mental-health-more-like-physical-health.html

Did you hear me wailing yesterday?

I wailed for you.

For all the times we've had, and even more the times that could've been.

I wailed from the deepest part of my being.

It was guttural and passionate and it emptied me.

I didn't know I could feel more empty.

And then it was silent.

I didn't know it could be more silent.

This books for you, Theo. Call it the counselling you'd always hoped I'd get.

It has helped.

For real.

Theo

RIOT

The sweltering Vietnamese sun bakes down on my pale skin as I sit curbside outside the Circle K, which is essentially a 7-11 with beer. The smell of motor oil and fresh-baked French breads from a patisserie down the way lighten my senses. I close my eyes and focus on the sounds of scooters and harsh Vietnamese accents that wash like a wave out of the marketplace. I can't believe we're really here! It feels like just yesterday that I dreamed up the idea of moving to Vietnam. My dad was in the war there, you see, so I felt there was so much I needed to experience for myself; opinions and judgements I needed to form on my own. On top of that, I wanted to practice teaching before becoming a fully certified teacher myself, and my boyfriend Theo had taught in Korea before I'd met him. To my delight, he agreed to join me.

On today's journey around Saigon we came to a very popular marketplace, bustling with vendors and Vietnamese families out for their afternoon shopping. We came to just look around and maybe buy a few trinkets for back home. Or so he thought...

All morning my stomach's been in knots. My temperature's been raised. My palms are sweaty. All morning I've been thinking about how much I love him. I am completely smitten with this man. We came to this place to start a new life; discarding most of our earthly possessions in exchange for a backpack and GPS. That's my favourite thing about this man: when adventure calls, he answers. Once we'd finished university in our hometown, we set off. "If we can survive this, we can survive anything," he'd say. And hell, we'd practically started living together from day one, drawn together by a force stronger than ourselves; I couldn't help but believe him.

All morning we've been walking through the market, and I still don't have the nerve. I want it to be perfect. The perfect proposal.

After six years what's really going to change? I ask myself continuously. Like a loop on replay, my mind wanders through the same questions. *Will we make it? Is he the right one for me? Can any marriage really last?* Holding my hand above my eyes to block the sun, I look over as Theo exits the Circle K, bringing with him a giant jug of cold filtered water. I didn't realize the thirst I'd built until looking at the glistening bottle. My throat tightens. I wring my hands and, before reaching for the condensation-covered clear plastic, blurt out, "Will you marry me?" His blue eyes sparkle, a grin forming inside his bushy red beard. Now I can't honestly remember what he said, but I know that our next stop was the jewellers down the alley. Two days later we had two rings beautifully crafted from silver and inlaid with a single strand of elephant hair, a symbol of luck and longevity.

We only stayed in Vietnam for three months, but we wore those rings for another two years, biding time by convincing family they were a hoax for the tight moral codes of Vietnam. "We couldn't get a hotel room together without them," we'd say. "They needed to think we were married". I guess we just weren't ready. Not ready to call it official anyways.

Fast forward another couple of years and we're on a quaint covered bridge above the Kuskanax River, rain pouring torrentially all around. It had been raining all weekend, in fact. Two dogs, three days of relaxing fun soaking in the Nakusp hot springs, and one mission by my man. I'd seen it coming since he asked me out of the blue to spend the weekend at our special place. The spontaneity reeked of some master plan. I'd seen it coming, but I still didn't know how I felt about it. I still didn't know what my answer would be. Well, of course, after eight years, I know what my answer will be...but is that an answer from both my head *and* my heart? Will there be fireworks? Will he get it right? Will I finally get my perfect proposal? The rain continues to pour down.

We went for one last walk with the dogs before the long journey home, my heart a little relieved he chose not to ask. Though it could've been romantic when the power went out in our little cabin and the front desk gave us two tiny tealights. Little did I know, and obviously he had forgot, he had stashed two grocery bags full of candles in the trunk of the car. His plan was to arrange them in a large heart and be waiting for me to return from a soak. His reality was to spend the weekend drenched, wait until the last possible moment of our trip, get me crying because I didn't want to go home and back to school, and turn as if he were offering me a piece of gum and ask..."Will you marry me?"

Now I shouldn't be so harsh. But there was no knee taken. No profession of love. I'm sure he was nervous as hell, but all I could say was "Why??!!," tears streaming down my cheeks. "Why wait till now? And will you please get on a knee?"

Of course I said yes, after a second attempt...but where was it? Where was my perfect proposal? I remember dreading telling my parents on the drive home. The fucking ring on my finger and I was still unsure we'd make it. Call me a perfectionist, but I always avoided the things I thought I may fail at. Marrying Theo was one of these unknowns. It scared the shit out of me. We were so compatible....but would we always stay that way?

When we get home I jot these and other thoughts into a new notebook I found at work (where I work with Theo): government-issued, plain, black, stark clear pages. This journal is eager for all my musings and non judgemental of my head games. It's the perfect place to pick apart and analyze the mountain of emotions growing inside of me. I spend the next year writing in deep contemplation in this notebook. *Am I ready to be married? I'm only 27. What if it doesn't work?* And on and on. No one but this book knows how afraid I am. It knows I dread planning a wedding and that the thought of all those people nearly paralyzes me while writing. It knows how I feel about Theo: the good, the bad, but mostly the ugly.

It knows I'm not ready...better than I know myself.

Fast forward one more year and the perfect proposal still weighs heavily on my heart. I've felt such guilt for my reaction to Theo's initial effort at the hot springs; I choose to make the responsibility mine again. So I get us on the road, giving him no clue where we may be headed. I arrange a cozy wood cabin, snacks for days, and a weekend of hot springing once again in our favourite place. This time I want the moment to be special, memorable, something to tell our kids about. I call ahead to the local chocolatier we always say we'll visit every time we're here, but never do. I arrange for them to write a note to be sneakily inserted in a box of chocolates we would buy. Once again, those four simple words: "Will you marry me?"

Fast forward to today. Theo and I don't talk. We haven't in over two years. And a piece of me feels hollow. It was after another year of being engaged that my fear of us failing began to eat at our seams. It invaded my thoughts constantly, and my journal grew thicker. I tried counselling and marriage-fixing audio books. I tried talking to Theo about it, my mom, and my friends. They all said it was normal to be nervous. But this was something more than nerves. I planned that wedding until I just couldn't anymore. And we split, ripped at the seams; a pair of pants now two legs lying limp. It felt like we'd failed before we'd even begun. And even though I initiated the breakup, I still felt unsure about my decision and afraid of what lay ahead on my own. Hell, I was eighteen when I met him and though I was a mature and independent thinker, I'd come to rely on him for so many of the basics in life. He was my partner in crime and my better half. I was terrified to stand on my own.

Looking back, I realize I've always had a boyfriend, in fact.

First there was Glen. We met as counsellors at bible camp when I was fourteen. And even though he lived in Alberta, we stayed strong and kept our promise of not kissing until our wedding day for the two years we dated! (Though we did many other things the Lord would likely not have approved of). Remember, that is the entire point of dating as a Christian...to be married. When we finally did kiss, I hated it....and we broke up shortly after. That's when I left the Christian faith and began to question everything I'd been told my entire life. I did a 180. I started dating an eighteen-year-old atheist I'd met at basketball camp, Drew. He was tall and hunky and we dated for two years as well...until he cheated on me.

Then I met Theo. One random day while working in the fish department at Safeway this bushy-faced man came up and started chatting to me about his history as a commercial fisherman. We talked for nearly an hour. He was so easy to talk to. When he left all I could think was *that was a really interesting older man*. We were nine years apart, you see, and I was nearing my nineteenth birthday when we met. When I saw him a few days later at TRU, our local university, I was quick to ask him for coffee. He walked me to math class and a few short hours later we were at Starbucks. That turned into Subway for dinner and then, as per my request, his house for a movie. I slept on his couch that night, and every night thereafter until I slept with him in his bed.

The one night I did return to my dorm room he joined me. We were fairly inseparable at this point. My bed was so small I ended up sleeping on the floor and leaving him to dream peacefully as I woke for my 6AM fish department shift. Shortly after, I ditched my dorm room completely and our life together really began.

But today things are different. We've broken up. And I have to cope. So I pack my things. I slough off years of accumulated crap. I take two chairs instead of four, DVDs instead of VHSs, and what bit of my sanity I can still sweep up off the floor. Yet, even when unladen of earthly goods and material possessions, fear of the unknown still runs through my veins, weighing me down, and at times holding me still in the universe. Not a calming kind of still, but the kind that paralyzes you.

Most of all, I feared being able to feed myself, as basic and unemotional as that may seem. He'd been the hunter and the cook for so many years. And I, a recent university dropout with no clear direction in life, found every decision (as simple as what groceries to buy) steeped in anxiety.

Now we need a bit of an interlude here to explain where this anxiety stemmed from. I'd never been an overly anxious person. But, as I mentioned earlier, failure terrifies me; it has all of my life. I've always been an overachiever and thus had little interaction with failure, and I liked it that way. I've always had a plan. And I've always clung to that plan as my sense of purpose in the world.

From a young age this purpose was to make a difference in the lives of others. I felt like I was put on this earth by God for a reason. At the age of twelve I began to manifest this into action. I was blessed enough to travel to Guatemala to work with the local people building churches and houses and basketball courts. I was blessed enough to see the reality of how the other half of the world lives. I was blessed enough to learn just how blessed I was as a young white woman living in Canada. It was then that I decided I wanted to use my privilege and knowledge to teach others less fortunate than myself, starting first in Guatemala, then on to East Hastings Street in Vancouver, BC, when I was fourteen, and finally, in the classroom both overseas and in Canada.

I always wanted to be a teacher, thinking it would be the perfect venue to manifest the gifts God had given me. I wanted to use the classroom to help others. That is, until I entered the classroom. Reality clicked in. Not only was I responsible for the health and safety of thirty children, I had their parents to keep happy, the school board to keep satisfied, and I actually had to instill knowledge!

During my teaching practicum I worked with kindergarten students. They wouldn't sit still, they pissed themselves, bit each other, and it was my responsibility to not only teach them the ABCs and 123s, but life skills and healthy relationship habits. I had to remember which ones fell off the playground that day, who was allergic to peanuts, and never mix up Calyn, Kallen, Kaitlyn, or Kale for fear of bruising their adolescent sensibilities. (I did, in fact, mix up a child's name one day. I think it was then that I knew I didn't want to teach. The look of distress in the little boy's eyes and the deep-seated sadness I knew I had caused was all too much.) The responsibility was too great.

Additionally - being a perfectionist - I allowed myself very little room for error. On top of that, I watched teachers spending thousands of their own dollars to better their classrooms, and thousands of their own hours to stay caught up with the workload. I had grown to like children less and less. And, at some point, I had shifted from an optimist to a realist.

So I dropped out.

Six years in.

Only one year left to complete my teaching certification, and I just couldn't do it. I couldn't lie to my principal, to my facilitators, and instructors...but most of all, I couldn't lie to myself. And though quitting was the most honest decision I could have made, it was also the most difficult thing I'd had to do in my life thus far. I'd put all my self-worth into my plan, and without it I felt like nothing. I was purposeless. I was useless. And I'd failed.

No decision seemed right anymore, no matter how much I contemplated it. An impending feeling of doom surrounded all my choices and plans of action. I started avoiding decisions entirely and places I would likely have to make decisions, like the grocery store I mentioned earlier. There would be so many people there, so many decisions to make, prices to compare, quality versus quantity, bulk versus boxed, bleached or unbleached flour—it was all too much. I'd spent the last few months curled up in bed avoiding life. I did not shop. I did not clean. I rarely bathed. I was deep in the depression and anxiety lay heavily upon me.

One day - while still dating, and when things had gotten especially bad with my depression - I called Theo to my bathroom, each of us having our own in our multi-floor townhouse. I'd been suffering for months and, like I said, not lifting a finger to clean. This, of course, included my toilet. I lifted the seat and gazed at my sludgy science experiment in the making. A long, stringy, kelp-like substance had begun to grow from the bottom of the bowl. I can distinctly remember the beautiful hues of green and turquoise turning to brown in the stringy kelp which sat atop a bed of lichen I bet Lysol was no match for…not that I would've tried even had it been. I remember calling Theo over to watch how it danced when I flushed the toilet.

He was disgusted.

I just laughed.

It was the most impressive thing I'd accomplished in months. And, having been cooped up for most of that time, probably the funniest. My laughter however wasn't without a hint of self-loathing; and disbelief that I'd let things get to such a point.

He tried to help, at first accommodating the depression, working around it, almost pretending—or rather hoping—it wasn't there. He read articles, talked to his close friends, tried to talk to me, and lastly begged me to seek help. I went twice and felt no better.

I wrote it off.

I often wonder how different my life would look if I'd kept going to counselling, if I'd had supports set in place, if I'd been ready for the tsunami that slowly ebbed closer, ominous, unseen, deadly. But I didn't. And once officially broken up, two years later, in December of 2017, my only concern became moving off of Theo's couch.

Because it was just that now:

His couch, no longer ours.

Amidst all the packing I found multiple journals - too many to keep, in fact - and decided to purge some of them. There was the beautiful Van Gogh spiral notebook I bought at Value Village fifteen years ago, the journal I made in high school graphics class, the recycled little brown book my grandmother gave me when I was fourteen - all of these too precious to dispose of. Then I found it: a simple black cover standard issue government notebook I took from the stationery room when I had first started working for the Ministry of Environment, where I worked alongside Theo.

It was such a sweet job.

When we'd moved here, it was for Theo's work with the government, and it didn't take long for them to hear word that I was also looking for employment. Not long after and they'd hired me to run the front desk of his office, encompassing three separate government ministries and over one hundred people, including Theo. Everyone in the ministry office used these plain black notebooks, and they were free to grab from the stationary room at any time. I figured I might as well discard the few used pages of the notebook I'd been filling and return it for someone else to use. (Now, I should explain that I journal frenetically. I'll pick any book, any page, and write when the musings come). In this particular book I only found a few pages at the front and a few at the back. I tore out the lists and doodles and returned the book to our shared office stationery room.

The stationery room I share with Theo.

Now after ten years Theo and I shared so much more than a stationery room. We shared lives, thoughts, dreams... though those now felt like illusions. We shared so much it seemed impossible to let it all stop. We couldn't turn it off. Though our love was fluid like water, our bodies connecting more deeply and sensually than they had in years, there was no proverbial tap to turn us off when we officially separated. There was too much love. Something about only seeing each other on a physical basis made everything so easy...or about a month.

Busy at work one day in our shared government office, my phone begins to vibrate on my desktop. I flip it over to see a picture message from Theo, and my heart drops. There it is. My worst fear realized: my plain, black, government-issued notebook. The words, "You might wanna burn this shit next time," below the picture.

He only sends one image, but it's enough.

A pros and cons list. Everything I love and hate about him, mostly the latter, no holds barred in vicious blue ink.

I call him immediately to explain, but it's no use...his phone is off, and the damage is done.

Then everything becomes cold. Even his words are icy to read. "Put my keys in my mail slot. The rest of your belongings bill be by the garage. Don't come to the house."

Nothing is so painful to the human mind as a great and sudden change."

— Mary Shelley, Frankenstein

sometimes the
hardest person
to walk away
from is the
person you've
always assumed
you were.

JmStorm

I know you're sad, so I won't tell you to have a good day. Instead, I advise you to simply have a day. Stay alive, feed yourself well, wear comfortable clothes, and don't give up on yourself just yet. It'll get better. Until then, have a day.

RIOT

Kelly

RIOT

Meet Kelly: my box dye, spray tan, *Bachelorette*-watching, Internet-dating new roommate. She must be in her forties or fifties, living alone in a two-storey house with her tiny dog, Tyke. I found her ad on Craigslist, of which there were very few, and we immediately bonded over a love of dogs. She seemed nice enough, though some red flags were raised when she began gossiping about her current roommate. Her eyes lit up with every juicy tidbit she divulged to me...a complete stranger. I shook it off. I took two rooms in the unfinished basement, paying more than her rent for the entire upstairs. But at this point, I'd take anything. I'd never been so desperate. Theo and I were still civil, the notebook not yet found, but things were wearing thin and I felt I'd nearly overstayed my welcome. I needed to leave before he had to ask me to. Kelly seems nice at first: cooking dinner to share, gifting my dog treats, offering her couch to watch smutty TV in the evening. I only sensed a touch of neurosis.

But as the month rolled along Kelly began to show her true colours. Texts over missing coffee mugs or a plate I may have taken down to my suite, lectures over how to wipe a counter, and the proper way to wrap up leftovers. Snide remarks if I used the microwave late after work, if I brought a friend over and we chatted too loudly...essentially, instructions for me that she never followed herself. It was all too much. Without my name on any lease, she was free to mistreat and control me any way she liked. And she knew I had no course of action other than to move out, so she continued to press. I couldn't live my life without her commenting on some part of it disapprovingly. I'd sleep till noon after a late shift at the pub and I was suddenly "depressed" and needed worrying over. I'd talk about Theo, and I was suddenly "weak" and needing a mind shift. I'd share anything and be stuck under a microscope of disapproval.

Never being one to roll over in a fight, I began to get crafty and creative to stay sane and keep some semblance of power. It started with her toothbrush travelling to the dark side—that's right, the dark side of my moon—then Nair hair remover in the shampoo, and bags of dog shit left on her porch. Anything spiteful I couldn't be pinned down for was fair game at this point. A little part of me had snapped. With no previous history of such maliciousness, I felt on fire and elated, as if I were following the true calling of my heart rather than simply stifling the pain and being the good girl I'd always been. I mean, I like to think I'm a very sweet human. Very sweet, until you fuck with me or someone I love. I was doing what I truly wanted to do for what felt like the first time. And it felt great!

After venting about my shitty living situation at work for weeks, one of my close friends and colleagues offered to provide a refuge.

I rented a U-Haul that very day, and confronted Kelly when she got home from work. My nerves were racing, but my heart was resolute. It wasn't pretty. Feeling too nice for my own good, I agreed to pay her a bit for the half month and had my U-Haul packed that night. I was on my way to freedom! She was pissed. She said she was going to talk to me about moving out, but never thought I'd be "one of those girls" to just up and leave. I just laughed, knowing I'd had my vengeance and been blessed with the better hand.

I spent two weeks living with my good friend and her family. Even though I found myself in another basement, I was surrounded by nothing but love and graciousness. I ate with the family, cleaned up the kitchen, bought groceries, drank coffee in the morning. One morning I even sat in the hot tub, overlooking all of Summerland, sipping a coffee, smoking a cigarette, as the snowflakes fell all around me. This was bliss...but I knew it had to be temporary.

I kept an eagle eye on the current rental listings. And soon enough, I found it: a home all my own. A mere ten-minute drive from town. A self-contained unit overlooking a vineyard with curvy walls, funky colours, and everything I needed within arm's reach. It was my first space just for me in nearly ten years. And it felt incredible...I never wanted to leave.

"It's not always just the heart.
Sometimes your mind breaks as well."

-R.H. Sin.

I like to think I am only mean to people who deserve it.

Kind of like a vigilant bitch.

A Bitchilante if you will.

facebook.com/WeirdPeopleRock

You gonna cry about it or boss up?

First of all imma do both.

Bill

RIOT

It's three in the morning and my friend Stephanie jumps on the back of a big white Harley. No explanation. No worries about the fact that I was supposed to drive us home after the bar, having never been much of a drinker. No nothing. The bike flares up and the street fills with the roar of Bill's double exhaust. My friend Stephanie is on the back now, hugging the biker's torso tightly, her skirt billowing on either side of the leather seat. At this point, I don't know Bill, and neither does Stephanie. But that doesn't seem to matter. His partner mounts his metal steed and they take off down Main Street, my fiery red Honda Fit following behind.

We reach Stephanie's boyfriend's house. He's conveniently gone for the week, so we set to cracking open the tequila. A few shots of Don Julio and we all become the best of friends. It's then that I find out I'm partying with a couple of Hells Angels. Stephanie turns up the music and heads to the kitchen with Bill's pal for another round.

It's just me and Bill.

He's big.

How did I not notice how big this man is?

His curly brown hair reaches past his shoulders, framing his flat facial features.

I can feel his eyes on me.

"Why you so gangster?" he asks abruptly, accusingly, but with a sparkle in his eyes. He catches me off guard, pinpointing my ghetto vein that often comes out while drinking. I start to use slang and swagger as if I'm from the hood. I think it's funny. I'm sure some people find it annoying. But, as with most people's opinions, I truly don't give a fuck. Without thinking, I challenge him, "Is that really a question we ask, Bill? You don't know where I've come from, what I've been through. Better question, why you so fucking gangster?" At this point I grab my drink, take a swig, and leap onto the couch behind him, dancing wildly. He chuckles. Satisfied by my swagger.

"Let's get a shot!" I declare.

I lead Bill to the kitchen and pour us a couple. The tart taste of lime bites at my tongue. We start bantering and before I know it I've jokingly punched him in the stomach….a stomach made of rock. Giggles quickly turn to fear at the realization I have just punched a Hells Angel, and I immediately start apologizing and tearing up. Bill just laughs.

The night continues into dawn and we retreat to the yard for fresh air and morning light.

Suddenly Stephanie's phone rings and her boyfriend angrily tells her the cops are on the way. Although we were loving the tunes, it turns out her early-rising neighbours were not. Bill and his comrade take to their Harleys, first grabbing a hug from each of us. And then they're gone with nothing left but a bit of dust and a ringing in my eardrums.

Later I receive a Facebook friend request from Bill and my heart drops. He's found me. I fear a little for my safety. *What does this Hells Angel want with me? Do I somehow owe him something? Have I made friends with the devil?*

I disregard my better judgement and click "Accept." *No sense hiding*, I think, *he's already found me.*

I am good, but not an angel. I do sin, but I am not the devil.

I am just a small girl in a big world trying to

find someone to love.

-Marilyn Monroe

Not everyone gets
the same version of me.
One person might tell you
I'm an amazing beautiful soul.
Another person will say
I'm a cold-hearted asshole -
Believe them both,
I act Accordingly.

Fuckology

Trevor

RIOT

Arms overloaded, I manage to open the heavy wooden doors of the tapas bar, instantly greeted with shrieks of wine-induced laughter. It's a small group tonight, but I can already tell they're going to be a handful. I drop the canvases on the table and my painting bag on the floor, taking a closer look at my participants. Two tables: one sits quietly partaking in appetizers and quietly chatting with one another, while the other - looking like they've been there for hours - indulges in a full-blown feast. The party table is surrounded by women, at least eight of them, and only one super buff, puffed chest, chiseled jawed beefcake of a man. I giggle under my breath, trying to sort out their situation. Am I teaching a polygamist group, is he their mascot, bouncer, personal security? I ponder all the possibilities while I set up their painting stations, inviting them over once I've finished. My first group comes immediately, glaring at the others who stay hovering over their bottle of red. I wait a few moments and try again. Finally, a simple, "Find your seats and shut up" does the trick. (I love injecting humour into my lessons. It's why I chose to teach adults and hated working with kindergartens. You can't tell a five year old to shut up, but you sure as shit can tell a drunk fifty year old…and I'll bet she giggles.)

I start my lesson with the usual placating of fears we all share when trying something new. Making art terrifies a lot of people apparently. We feel as though we have to do something "right" and can't let go of that inner critic. I learned never to start a class by asking, "Who's an artist here?," because no one will look you in the eye, and you'll have lost their confidence forever. My typical routine is to ease my students into a creative headspace, coax out their inner artist, and set them free from fear to simply enjoy their night. "We are our own worst critics. Try to be kind to yourself. Just play. Now everybody take a sip." I finish, grabbing my paint brush like it was a sword and I was about to lead my troops into battle. I look out and catch one soldier still standing, formidable and solid, arms crossed, a stern look across his face. "Who is this guy? Ex-military?" I inquire to the group in jest, his posse laughing hysterically. "Yo Sarg, Captain, whatever, take a seat it's time to paint!" He chuckles, his big arms puffing further from his chest, as he sits in amongst his girl squad.

I get the first blobs of paint onto the canvas and start circling the room to check on my troops. Arriving at the party table I can't help but ask, "So what's going on here?" The women burst into giggles and Trevor's well-constructed grin widens. I hear someone say "trainer" and finally put the puzzle together. These women have brought their gym trainer to a painting class. We all laugh and then I zero in on Trevor, asking "How do you like being a trainer?" With no hesitation he responds, "I fucking love it. You tell 'em to hit the deck, put their asses in the air, and they do it!" I feel my cheeks reddening and I know—it's on. The attraction is real.

Now, just a little back story: Theo and I still hook up (he hasn't yet found the journal). But since officially breaking up, I've had sex in my car, in a married man's bed (I didn't know he was married at the time), and with my married friends. I'd become a new woman. Growing up Christian, I had certain hang ups about sex, and had never been one for casual encounters. Theo and I stopped having sex before we broke up, and to be honest I'd grown quite square about it all. I'd lost touch with my sexuality and, in turn, touch with myself. At first I was shocked by my openness. I was shocked at how deeply I sunk into the sensual pool of my own sexuality. I became brave about sex. I learned to embrace it. Then I pursued someone in a position of authority over me, my roller derby coach. I pursued him just to see if I could, and while of course I was attracted to him, I was also curious to see just how potent my sexuality had become. He agreed to a date and told me he's polyamorous, his honesty and forthrightness about it all such a breath of fresh air. There was no shame. No hiding any truths from anyone. Each relationship had its own special circumstances. I didn't need to be everything for this man. Neither should I expect him to meet all of my needs. It just made so much sense. A man to fuck when I want to fuck, another to snuggle and maybe some nights just shoot the shit. If one's not around, I've got another on speed dial. I am a freshly single, sexy, twenty-something...why should anything hold me back from getting everything I want?

That night I flirted with the hunky man surrounded by women in the quaint little tapas bar. I spent extra time making sure the painting for his mother came out just right, and gave him just enough glances and glowing remarks to let him know I was interested. All night we flirted back and forth.

When the class was over, his girl squad invited me to smoke a joint outside the restaurant, pre legal cannabis. He does not imbibe, telling me he's an ex-cop, but has no problems with people that do. My like for this man grows stronger. Finishing up, he starts walking toward their van to head back to Osoyoos, an hour away.

"Don't you want my number?" I ask.

He beams.

We chat for days.

Over the next month there are few days I don't see Trevor. He travels an hour to see me for the evening, before training at 6am. I travel an hour to see him in between his sessions. We click immediately. So much so that I crack the news to my other suitors. I don't want to juggle three men. I can see it going big with Mr. Man and I don't want anything interfering.

I know this breaks Theo's heart, but at this point I don't care. Sure, we've been still seeing each other in some regard, but I've become detached. And I feel like I've truly moved on. I am a newer, fresher me. More resolute about what I want and empowered by the amazing paths life is putting before me. I have never felt sexier, more in control, or more excited for the adventures ahead. I'm a newly single young woman, dating a gorgeous older man who treats me like gold. I feel like candy on his arm, and it feels good. He shows me off, brings me to his bar, introduces me to his training clients. I am in my prime.

I feel such elation I decide to commemorate this newfound freedom with some newfound ink.

Now, as I've said, roller derby is where I acquired the name Riot. And during all of this chaos with Theo it seems I've been living up to my name on the track. So far I've been given two official warnings from the team captain within less than a month. Now I can't honestly remember what these warnings were for, but from day one this teams been too prude for my liking: parties ending at 9PM, unanswered calls to my Caviar Can for tequila shots after a big bout, little room for wiliness in a sport bred in the underground and known for being badass. Hell, I'd throw a solid hit in practice and nearly be condemned for being too violent. Even my friends were scoped out, and nearly thrown out of a game for handmade signs saying "fucking Riot" in big bedazzled letters. And then there was the time I threw up the middle finger in a bout and all hell broke loose. It was all so PG, such a joke!

The team gathered together and decided to host a sort of tribunal in my honour, telling me a mere couple of days before in an email that I was at risk of suspension and could come defend myself if I wished.

I felt such a connection to my alter ego, to Riot, that no matter what league I was in (having been in two at this point and played alongside multiples as a pickup) I would forever be Riot. No overarching umbrella, league, team, whatever you wanted to call it, was going to define me. I defined me. So fuck 'em.

And so I called the local tattoo shop in Osoyoos.

She had a one hour window.

I took off as fast as I could.

"Oh shit. You want all four knuckles?!"

My heart sank.

"I don't need anything fancy! You can even do it free hand if you like. Just typewriter font, about this big, 'R.I.O.T'."

She agreed... a little doubtfully.

We looked up some fonts on her computer and then it was go time.

Now, this moment was pretty wild, guys. My theme song had become Let's Start a Riot by Three Days' Grace, and I played it over and over and over. Somehow it helped me feel more powerful and secure in this person I was becoming. I was changing. That much was clear, even to myself. I was building opinions, where once I'd just gone along with Theo's. I was building a backbone where once I was weak. I knew what I stood for and I wasn't afraid to fight for it. I asked the tattooist, "Do you mind if I sing while you tattoo?" "Sure thing," she replied.

I pressed play on my phone.

Honestly, I don't think she knew what was coming her way. And I bet she still tells the story of tattooing a Riot's knuckles. Because, in a voice I'd never heard from my own body, let alone that of a demon's—something much more like a growl than a singing voice—I *sang* Let's Start a Riot. Every bit of pain I felt tremoring through my knuckles, the pinching, and seething warm agony; every bit of that torture I snarled out in that song.

I stopped *singing* at one point and demanded she stop as well.

"Stop! I can't take it!"

"Sorry. Can't. In the middle of a letter."

I growled directly at her.

This happened to occur on the "I" of "RIOT" and, looking back at it now, it is rather poetic, really. The riot that was happening was not the door-crashing, window-smashing, grand theatrics you may expect from a typical riot. This riot was more symbolic, even subtle perhaps. There was a shift happening. There was a riot within myself...within the proverbial "I." *I wanted to make a difference. I wanted to defy the rules. I wanted to be seen and heard.*

So I snarled that song until both her needles and the beat of the song stopped simultaneously....I'm not shitting you....the exact same moment.

I'd always thought that knuckle tattoos were too hardcore for me: the girl who planned all her tattoos to be concealable for teaching in the classroom. But somehow there was no question. R.I.O.T. knuckles. That was it. And tattooed "upside down" as someone put it one day. "It's for me to read," I explained. All of my tattoos are highly personal and hold deep meaning, but there was something different about this one. Not only was I commemorating my life as a roller derby badass, I was proclaiming something to the world. No matter how personal the tattoos felt, there they were, plain as day, on my knuckles....R.I.O.T. for all the world to see. I still think about my eighty-year-old self sporting R.I.O.T. knuckles and I giggle. Honestly, that's the type of woman I'd want to be friends with, and I take pride in that.

Some people don't understand, or care to take the time to. I've branded myself a rebel, "a violent disturb[er] of the peace"[3]. I see the looks. And I don't care. Quite honestly, I sort of hate people. Why not give them a reason to leave me alone?

Trevor, aka Mr. Man seems unsure of my choice.

---
[3] Oxford dictionary

Theo notices them one day in the office and seems excited I'm coming into my own again. I gotta say, that man was always supportive of my personal growth, and to this day I don't speak ill of his presence in my life. Sure, he may feel like I "wasted [his] time," but I still remember, learn, and grow from our experiences together. And I hope I always will.

Any who, carrying on. Mr. Man likes to buy me things and make me feel special. He takes me to fancy restaurants I've only heard of. At one point he promises to name his boat after me and let me paint it. I hear word of his airplane and we visit his hangar space. He takes me to the US for Mexican food and cheap gas, and I get to hold an AK-47 while standing in his lifted truck listening to country music and smoking a doobie. This is the life! I am his own "Private Riot" as he called me, and I feel high on happiness.

That is...until the night he physically abused me.

And while small in gesture, I sensed a sick demented pleasure in my pain. We had been full of passion, both between the sheets and in our fights. We had had our share of yelling matches and stand-offs. I once threw food in his face, he threatened to leave me across the border, nearly hit me with his lifted truck, and on and on. He even had his whole pub turn on me; employees bullying me after shift, stalking me, scaring me so much I called the cops one night to escort me back to Trevor's (having no idea he'd been behind it all). He liked the power struggle, always assuming he'd come out on top. Not surprisingly, this Riot got the best of the ex-cop more often than not, as most riots do. I'd surprise him at his pub, casually sitting and sipping a beer without him even noticing my entrance. He was the bouncer...his only job was to notice my entrance. Or the night he handcuffed me and "lost" the keys; I was out the door, sitting in the grass, smoking a cigarette so casually when he got back from the truck moments later. I loved to outsmart him! Something in me thrived on the drama, and instead of running for the hills like the good girl I'd been, I kept going back for more.

This physical abuse was something new. I've never been one to be pushed around. And sure, he apologized profusely, but things weren't the same after that. I became hyper-paranoid. And I *mean* hyper-paranoid! I hid in my house, often crouched behind the couch watching out the window for Trevor's truck or his Porsche or any vehicle with someone who looked like Trevor in it. I barricaded myself in, cluttering all sorts of junk outside my front door so I would hear intruders. I was convinced he was going to come hurt me.

Then he called one day and confessed to cheating on me with his ex. There was no remorse. No sympathy or empathy or care for my feelings at all. There was little intonation in his voice. He sounded like a sociopath. I peppered him with questions about all the gory details, wanting him to feel something for all the things he was making me feel.

"Where'd you fuck her?"

"My truck."

"How many times?"

"I dunno."

"Did you do it in my seat or in the back?"

"Why do you want to know all this?"

"Because I feel like you fucking killed her and left her body stashed in the woods somewhere you sick fuck!"

He laughs. And all I can do is think of her soft flesh still steaming in the ditch of some back road.

It wasn't something I had expected from Mr. Man, but the longer I knew him, the less I liked him. The more I looked in his eyes, the more crazy I saw. The more I trusted, the more reasons he gave me to distrust.

Smash, one of my best roller derby buddies who also lived in Osoyoos, had become my wing-woman for all adventures south of Penticton and privy to all things Trevor. The timeline of our relationship echoed mine and Mr. Man's. Smash joined the league around the same time I met him. She knew our team wouldn't like her either…. "Too prudish," she'd say, "I'm too wild for this crowd." We had so much fun together…Smash'ing Riots, stirring up all the shit in Osoyoos (hell, it's a retirement town….needs a little shaking up!) Somehow, however, Smash forgot to tell me the night Trevor made a move on her.

It was during the great flood of 2018, the biggest in 200 years in the Okanagan. With a house two feet underwater, Trevor and I found ourselves staying in a hotel room, playing house for the week. Smash came over one night. We went to his pub, got trashed, and I ended up in the bathtub of the hotel room…my safe haven when I've had a few too many wobbly pops. I can remember feeling such trust; my new man, my new best friend, cuddled in bed together waiting for me. Nothing would happen. I was so sure of it, so trusting of them both. Apparently I was wrong. While I laid soaking, water beating on my bloated drunk belly, Trevor decided to make a move on my best friend. And not only make a move, but full-blown stick his dick in her face! She thought it best to not tell me as she didn't "want to ruin a man's life." *But what about my life*, I thought. She let me keep pursuing the creep for over a month, putting me in danger. I couldn't believe it! And instead of being scared or sad, I got angry. Our friendship was over….and I was going to ruin this man's life, without her help! How could he? I'd been so honest about the other men I was seeing. And I'd left them in the dust when things started getting serious with us. Why couldn't he be honest with me? I could've shared. Three friends in a hotel bed sounds like a decent time to me. But he was just a creep—a creep to his core. And it wasn't about love or trust or connection, it was about power and domination and deception.

Enraged, I took action. I left notes outside his work, attempted to smash the windows out with rocks, texted relentlessly, and stopped by his home to rage from the street.

I acted like a crazy woman! I did things you only see in movies and wish you'd be confident enough to do in real life. Somehow I was confident enough. It was like something had taken over me. I didn't fear authority, I just wanted vengeance. Unfortunately, for the sake of not completely incriminating myself, I can't divulge all of my creative wiles. But I'll let you pontificate what you might do in my situation. Then times the intensity by three and you're probably at my level.

I can remember arriving at his house in the black of night. Going to his back sliding glass door as sneaky and cocky as can be one evening. I stared at him lying on the couch, the couch we'd just been snuggling on days earlier. I remember staring at the back of his head, wondering what would happen if I tapped the glass. Who could get to the gun in his bedside table quicker?

I'm thankful I never tapped.

At this point I don't know what I would've done had I won that race.

But I did so many other things I'd only dreamed of doing in this situation. It was invigorating, especially when the ex-cop, bouncer, trainer, wanna-be city councilman, Trevor convinced the police I was the problem and the Boys in Blue started stalking me. They met me, lights swirling, outside any bar I visited in Osoyoos. They met me after the bar. They met me before the bar. One night we'd had so many meetings, I decided to evade another and grabbed Leo and went walking toward Trevor's. We took off, ducking from tree to tree, keeping in the shadows to avoid the swirling red, white, and blues. Thankfully it was a bit of a walk, because by halfway there I decided it better for Leo and I to sleep it off and return to our Caviar Can in the morning. I spotted a bridge with some soft smooth stones underneath and decided to nestle into a ball to hide from the whipping wind. I slept under that bridge, clutching my small scruffy puppy, my best friend and partner in crime, tightly in my arms all night. That was the day I gained a real sense of empathy for the homeless.

I felt like a criminal on the run. It was like they had GPS on my car, tracking my every movement. I could almost hear their radios start chattering every time I drove down the hill into Osoyoos. I wanted to tell them what he'd done to me, but I knew their minds were already made up. He was the victim; I, the villain.

Looking back at it now... maybe they were right.

"People are not born heroes or villains;

they're created by the people around them."

-Chris Colfer

Jun. 19, 2018

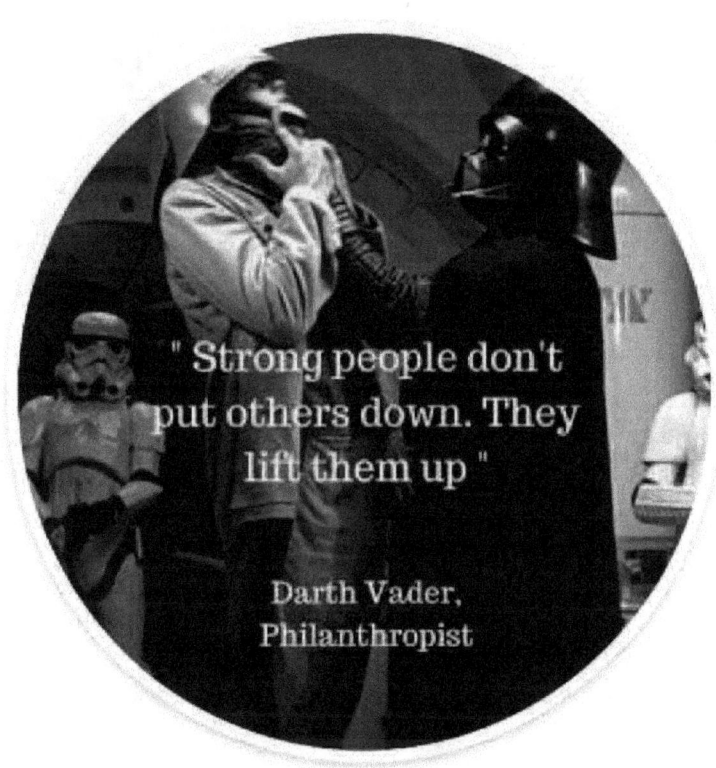

I NEVER want 2 be the raging bull dyke who hates men.....

But jaaaaazuuussss, I see very fucking clearly why some women go down that road

Fack. Life.

#riot
#rioton
#riotlove
#riotmakers
#riotriotriot
#riotagainsthate
#riothard
#riotagainstrape
#riotonbitches
#riot
#riot
#riot

#love
#lovealways

#fuckmen
#fuckrapists
#fuckhate

CLAIRE

Remember Bill, my Hells Angel acquaintance? Well at this point we've become good buddies. We go for beers and ride our motorbikes together. He even lets me lead a pack of Hells Angels one night en route to Kelowna. Let me tell you, the rush of riding a motorbike is heightened a hundred fold when you've got some of the most badass men and their women following your every move. We'd blow by semis, make our own lanes of traffic; in short, we ruled the road and I knew Bill had my back.

I tested that theory one day.

Bill liked to go slower than I did, so while he kept pace a few cars back I would bomb along for some adrenaline and then slow back down to meet him. Well we'd just passed Penticton and this dumb bitch in a shitty little car is putting along in the fast lane (my biggest of pet peeves). I roar up behind her, and nothing. She refuses to move over. So I start to hightail her ass, my adrenaline pumping as my anger rises. I tighten the squeeze on my handlebars and rev a little closer. *We rule the road!* Finally she shifts over and then all hell breaks loose. The stupid bitch throws me the finger, and fuck has she messed with the wrong woman on the wrong day! Feeling all powerful with a Hells Angel riding thirty feet behind me in a black skull face mask, I grab up Slim, my crowbar, from between my handlebars. I shake it violently at her, so tempted to smash out her windows, swerving closer and closer, screaming that she doesn't know who she's messed with. All of a sudden Bill's behind me, waving his arms for me to stop. That was the day Bill stopped riding with me. I was too much of a "heat score" (aka dumbass) and he didn't want to get caught.

Regardless, he knows what Trevor's been putting me through and I completely believe he wants to help. "It's $5,000 to break an arm, $10,000 a leg" he tells me one day over a couple of brews. "I don't want him dead. But I want to watch him squirm" is all I say back.

One night Bill invites me to his house for a small gathering. There's surveillance cameras surrounding the house, tall fences, and multiple motorbikes parked in front.

These are the things I remember:

- Everyone else started drinking early in the night, so I grabbed a 2-6 with probably five shots of vodka left...that's it!

- Not feeling very social, I took myself downstairs to drink and rap with Tech Nine on their big screen TV. The song "Riot Maker" and Three Days Grace "Let's Start a Riot" changed my life during this time. I would sit watching the lyrics scroll by, my tongue working overtime to stay caught up, for hours. The lyrics and heavy beats spoke to my inner Riot, coaxing her out.

- Bill's cousin Claire comes down and confronts me, wanting me to go outside. She was moving into the basement the next day, and she started to get territorial; demanding I leave.

- Enraged, I head upstairs to finish my drink and rap to myself.

- I wake up on the couch and take myself for a shower.

- The cops enter the bathroom, remove me from the shower, and take me to their squad car.

These are the things I'm told:

- I drank the vodka.

- I got naked alone upstairs.

- Bill walks in.

- I am violently beating myself and screaming at no one.

- He tries to stop me, but I use my fiery red acrylic talons to scratch him off of me.

- I expose all parts of my body aggressively, pulling at my thighs and breasts, screaming, "I'll hurt myself before I ever let you hurt me, Trevor."

- I manage to get away from Bill.

- I exit their house and run into the street stark naked, still screaming.

- I mount my motorbike and lay back into a power pose. (This part I remember the next morning as I notice my mirrors are slanted sideways)

- Bill somehow manages to get me back in the house and wraps me in a blanket on the couch.

- I wake up on the couch and take myself for a shower.

- Claire hears me turn on the shower and calls the police.

- The cops enter the bathroom, remove me from the shower, and take me to their squad car.

I hear the loud bang at the bathroom door, "POLICE!" I immediately burst into tears, unsure of what I've done. The shower curtain pulls open and I'm completely exposed to the butch female officer. *She's kind of cute*, I notice. She helps me from the tub, two male officers in the hallway, and brings me to my backpack to pick out clothes. I choose booty shorts and my roller derby jersey. We make our way to the squad car and then onto the station. I can think of nothing I've done wrong.

They bring me into processing and I must remove all of my jewellery. Heavy bangles, a handful of rings, and a few necklaces make their way into a large clear bag. (Somehow the more jewellery I wore, the more powerful I felt. Sort of like Wonder Woman with her fierce bracelets.) I'm made to face the wall, arms spread, and they search me for weapons and contraband, thankfully never making me squat and cough! (Not that I was hiding anything, it just seems like a degrading experience I was happy to avoid).

I'm then led to a cell with nothing but a stainless steel sink, toilet, and a heavy sliding door.

I spend what feels like hours circling the room, crouching in the warm spots, trying to heat up my exposed skin. It's freezing in this cell and I wonder who dressed me. *Such an idiot*, I think, forgetting I'd chosen my own clothes. I'm still drunk. I begin hammering on the door, screaming for a blanket, food, and maybe an explanation of why I'm in here. I take my best roller derby stance and hammer on the door over and over until someone finally arrives. "It's so cold! Could I please have a blanket?" The face remains emotionless in the window and then he walks away.

I'm becoming desperate for heat and notice the sink has a hot water button. One punch and the water runs for around five seconds. It's warm and soothing on my frozen hands. I begin bathing my arms and my legs. But as soon as I stop the cool air whips my skin harder than before. Finding it easier, I climb up into the sink and continue pushing the button and bathing. I do that for so long my acrylics begin pulling away from my nail beds. I begin ripping them off one by one, debating how I could use them as mini sharpened weapons against a guard. I have so much time for my mind to wander.

I take to banging on the door again and screaming, my shoulders and biceps aching with each blow. "You're all about the old school derby," my coach used to tell me unimpressed, "Big hits aren't everything." And, while not a compliment (in his eyes), I harnessed all the rage, confusion, and aggression I could muster and slammed on the door as if it were every big bitch I'd ever met on the track. No one was going to determine my worth anymore. No one was going to tell me what to do. And no one was going to keep me locked up!

With no reply, I decide to try some of the tricks I've learned from my favourite prison TV shows. I pretend to smash my head on the wall over and over wailing in pain. I lay out motionless as if hurt. This does nothing. Completely unabashed at this point, I remove my jersey, breasts exposed, and shove it violently into the toilet. If they won't listen to me, they'll sure as shit listen to a flood. "FLUSH!" the toilet begins to fill and then stops. "FLUSH!" No more water runs. They've seen this trick before.

"Why'd you do that?!" a voice bellows from the small glass window. "Because I'm cold and hungry and don't know why I'm in here!" He stares for a moment and then continues down the hallway again. I can hear laughing from under the door.

Solemnly, I climb back into the sink and sit with my thoughts. If I did nothing to end up in here this must all be a ploy. There must be something else going on; someone protecting me, keeping me locked away so I can't be found, or better yet blamed. I made it clear I didn't want Trevor killed—just roughed up a little. Hell, I don't have $5,000 an arm or 10,000$ a leg. I was hoping these guys would work for hugs and good intentions.

I begin to rest more easily knowing I'm in here for a purpose. I'm protected. And they can't keep me locked up forever. Bill and his buddies are trained criminals; they'll get the job done quickly.

I shift my butt into the curve of the sink, perched three to four feet in the air, and begin to doze.

Finally the heavy door slides open and an officer steps in. I pull my damp jersey from the toilet, over my body and follow them into an office, pleading for a glass of water. I realize how stupid I must seem, spending hours warming my body in a sink I could've also been drinking from. The water is so cold and clean tasting.

We settle into the office and I inquire about why I've been incarcerated. The officer checks his records and concludes that the caller, Claire, said I drank two full 2-6s of vodka. He tells me no further details, but I'm enraged at the lie, having no recollection of the real series of events.

I ask him for a ride back to Bill's, having no idea where I am. We wait on the steps. I'm an emotional wreck. I crumple to my knees when Bill opens the door. Leo comes scurrying toward me and I burst into tears. Apparently his cousin, Claire, wanted to send Leo to the pound last night, and I can't thank Bill enough for saving him. We spend the day piecing together our timelines, until I'm convinced that Trevor is fine and everything else was an enraged drunken blackout. I've never blacked out before in my life, and I've certainly drank more than five shots of vodka. This was something different, something powerful and terrifying. Something mental and imbalanced. Some trigger or switch that was flipped in anger and agitated by alcohol. I pack up my belongings, settle Leo into the saddle bag, and set off on my motorbike, Foxy Freedom, never to see Bill again.

"Here's to alcohol, the cause of, and solution to, all life's problems."

-The Simpsons

 Jul. 17, 2018

So #RIOT officially is a jailbird....!!!!!!!!!!!!

Let that settle in.....

....

....

...

Best guess why gets you a #riothug delivered personally by yours truly

(Please friends, this is no joke and I am about 2 post some very very serious and personal things in the next couple of days for the sake of educating the masses. If you haven't heard from me in a while....youll soon know why)

Light and love 2 you all.
Xoxo

RIOT

Jul. 27, 2018

I don't know
where I'm going
from here
but I promise
it won't be
boring

-David Bowie

RIOT

Aunty Cheryl

RIOT

She keeps nattering on about how much fun we can have. And honestly, the more she talks, the dumber she looks to me. And the dumber she looks, the angrier I get. I don't really know why I'm so mad. Just that I am.

Stupid bitch keeps suggesting a lemon vanilla cake, clearly not knowing my mother at all.

I know my mother!

"And we can bake it together...have fun decorating it...it'll be great!"

I scoff, completely agitated.

The more she speaks the more I want her to leave.

Why she'd even come, I'll never know. Hell, I can't remember the last time my mother had something nice to say about Aunty Cheryl, or some positive memory to recollect and share. It had always been a tumultuous relationship. And I honestly felt like I barely knew the woman standing in my mother's kitchen.

Picture this.

You feel a need to escape where you are for whatever reason. Right now, it felt like I was escaping for all the reasons.

Where do you go that's safe?

...you go home.

That's where you go.

So I pointed the nose of the Caviar Can North, Mr. Leo in tow, and set off on the epic sixteen hour journey to Smithers to see my family. Hell, I'd been bopping from island to island, mainland to the Sunshine Coast, back to the Okanagan a few times for supplies, all within a couple months, so what's one more road trip? At this point my car is most definitely my home. It's my safe space, organized an reorganized daily to meet every need that may arise. It's my thumping speaker system when I just need to rock out, and it's my wheels when I need to quickly scoot from a compromising situation. It's where I snuggle in at night, or some nights at least, and it's where I watch my Netflix and chill- typically in a McDonalds parking lot. It's my Caviar Can; fancier and more expensive than a tuna can. And it's going to take me and my tiny pup north to the safety net of home.

Mom was in Haida Gwai in a pre-celebration of her fiftieth birthday, and due home in a few days. Unknown to me, was that her sister had travelled from Alberta and was also planning on surprising her for her birthday

I remember feeling very defensive. This was *my* parent's house. *I* needed them right now, and I definitely didn't want some other woman stealing my mother's attention.

So, despite her genuine attempts to bond with me - her niece she hadn't spoken to in years – I decided to give nothing but backlash. And instead of making her precious lemon vanilla cake, I was going to get something my mother would actually enjoy. So I travelled into Smithers and bought every piece of gawdy over priced 50th birthday crap I could find at the local dollar store. Then I bought a small black forest cake, her real favorite, and just big enough for her and I to share. I asked my sister who lived next door if I could borrow their tiny cabin in their back forty to host this very special party with just my mom and I.

So, my mom arrives home. Apparently, unbeknownst to me at the time, my aunt has texted my mother warning her that we've had a confrontation and that I don't seem myself.

Aunty Cheryl makes her own birthday cake for mom. And as with so many of my grandiose plans these days, I flake out...big time. I never host the special surprise birthday in the woods I had so extravagantly planned. I don't hang the fiftieth birthday streamers, or make her wear the sash, or even eat the cake! I still don't know where the cake went in fact. I thought I'd dropped it out of the car when unloading the birthday goodies, and then figured maybe I drove over it the next day, but there was no evidence at all! No broken plastic, no cherries or icing, no dogs sick from eating too much chocolate cake...nothing. Had I even bought a cake? Nothing seems certain right now.

If not for the plastic bag full of cheap party favors, it's as if my mother's birthday never existed in my life at all. Someone so special to me, and I can't even follow through on celebrating her...I was so caught up in myself.

I hop between my sister's (who lives next door, approximately one kilometer away) and my parent's. With aunty Cheryl taking the downstairs for her and her son to sleep, I can't honestly remember where I ended up night after night. But I know I used my car to escape. Just as I'd been doing for months now. Things get tense, I hit the road, usually with a 6pack beside me.

One day I decide to clean out the Caviar Can, and left two full trash bins of empty cans and liquor bottles at my sister's, my meager collection from the past weeks' driving.

Mom and I go for a drive one morning and she asks what I'm drinking from my coffee mug. I tell her it's clamato juice...which isn't a complete lie.

We cruise the back roads aimlessly, talking about everything. This is one of my favorite memories of my mom and I; One of my favorites of my life thus far. I remember feeling supported, listened to, and finally like an adult accepted by my mother while I drove. Yes, I was choosing to drink and drive. I lived in my car at this point. And lately I really liked to drink, more so now than ever before in my life. What more can I say?

But this trip brings flashbacks to when I was sixteen and learning to drive, feeling completely unsupported by my mother as she gripped the door handle in terror every time I got behind the wheel. This feeling was the complete opposite. I sat, beer and calmato in one hand, cigarette in the other, and the steering wheel clutched somewhere in between. Mom sat casually beside me. Gripping nothing. No fear. Just listening….and cruising with me, something I'd been doing for months straight now.

I can't remember much from this trip, except that I was searching from something I couldn't find. I was searching for peace. And I thought escaping the Okanagan, being with my closest people- my family- I thought that would fix everything. Turns out, I was wrong.

My aunt left Smithers before I did, and I was so happy to have my family back to myself. I was hoping for some alone time with my favorite people.

So me and my dad are sitting at the table one morning shooting the shit, smoking a cigarette, and drinking some coffee…our typical way to start the day. I should explain beforehand that tensions are always a little high when it's just my dad and I. He's stubborn and obstinate…and, so am I. So sometimes we clash. And sometimes I choose not to share personal stories for fear of us clashing. Well, this morning I let my guard down and admit to some sadness and frustration I'd been feeling for losing Theo, a topic I am always very leery to discuss with him. As melodramatic as it may sound, I'd always had a sensitivity about my dad and Theo. Whether he'd ever admit it or not, it was clear that he liked Theo. He liked him a lot. It got to the point that I felt he liked Theo more than me., his daughter.

So this morning, with no one else to vent to, I turn to my dad.

Now I can't remember exactly what I said, but- predictably- my dad took sides with Theo.

"Just leave him alone daughter. You've done enough."

"Excuse me?! What about what he's done to me?!"

He continues to side with Theo, my frustration rising and turning to rage (something that was becoming more and more common for me these days).

I remember looking him dead in the eye…

And slowly letting the words drip off my tongue.

"Fuck you!!"

They rolled with such purpose and oozed with vehemence.

I grabbed my dog and my keys and went storming to the car.

I could feel his eyes watching me from the upstairs window.

While my mother had a growing concern something was wrong with me, my dad tried to disregard it, believing my mother to be overreacting. That's just the way it goes sometimes, we don't want to believe the worst, especially of those we know the best.

I took off immediately and drove into Smithers to visit mom one last time at work, explaining that we'd been in a fight and I didn't want to stay in town anymore.

She understood and apologized.

I can't imagine how she must have felt. Knowing something was internally wrong with her daughter and the man she loved agitating her into leaving their home. She told me later she thought it might be the last time she saw me.

I kissed her forehead. Told her I loved her. And pointed the Caviar Can south.

Nowhere feels safe.

And I am the only one whose got my back. That much is clear.

I feel lonelier than ever.

But I *will* find peace.

I'll drive, and run, and flee till I find it.

I know it's out there somewhere.

Mom's Notes:

"When Chelsea came to visit at the end of June I could see yet again, things were very off. She was drinking heavily, easily agitated and fixated on the 'wrongs' friends and Theo had done her.

The visit ended up in a fight with her dad and her leaving our home. I was terrified where she was going to end up. We texted/spoke daily for which I'm so grateful."

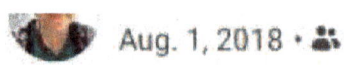 Aug. 1, 2018

All seasons 4 reasons

Hold strong #riotmakers and #rioton!!

#riot
#riotlove
#riotrambles

THERE IS PURPOSE IN THIS SEASON
THERE IS PURPOSE IN THIS SEASON
THERE IS PURPOSE IN THIS SEASON
THERE IS PURPOSE IN THIS SEASON
THERE IS PURPOSE IN THIS SEASON
THERE IS PURPOSE IN THIS SEASON
THERE IS PURPOSE IN THIS SEASON

Chris

RIOT

I'm wearing the blue fleece robe Theo bought me for Christmas last year over my floral-patterned cocktail dress, screaming at the top of my lungs in downtown Vancouver. Everyone is wearing one of my coats or sweaters from my car actually. And what's left, but the blue fleece robe for the queen, yours truly, little miss Riot. Chris continues to piss me off, pestering me about sharing my tequila with the straggling bar crowd I invited back to my car. Despite the fact that we drove at least forty kilometers per hour over the limit the whole way here, my friend Sarah and I arrived at 2AM, just in time to watch the Granville Street dance floors close down. Chris met us there and I took off, leading the way through the crowds. I love the after the bar scene! Everyone's tipsy, messy, and in no hurry to head home. Granville Street is barricaded off by police, as humans are everywhere. Some of the food vendors play music and Sarah and I dance in the streets. I feel so alive! I'm ready to take this city by storm. I meet a few people and invite them back to my Caviar Can, not noticing that they're all men.

Chris notices.

I met Chris at a pool tournament over a year ago while I was having a drink out one day. He's one of the best pool players in BC. We stayed in touch over the year and last month I decided to reach out on my trip to Victoria, where he lives. Although I had friends to stay with, I found myself most nights at Chris's. He took me dancing, cooked me food, and made sweet raunchy love to me. It was a week of bliss.

When I messaged about coming to Vancouver I think Chris expected more than being a dancing partner.

Flashback to my blue robe. Chris continues to make a fool of himself, regardless of the fact I've already taken him aside to explain how inappropriate his behaviour is. He's acting like a child, and I now find myself screaming at him to piss off in front of everyone. He wants a drink. I tell him to go for a walk first to calm down. He continues harassing me. "Walk it!" I scream. Then again, "Walk it!" over and over, as the eyes of my guests widen at the drama. It feels liberating. Albeit frustrating. "Walk it!" I shriek one last time.

By the end of the night I've punched a metal sliding door, taken off jogging in my cocktail dress, and tried to hide in my car pretending to sleep in the hotel parking lot. Many people come to my car window wanting to party, but I keep *sleeping*, clutching Leo tightly to my chest, buried under a towel in the front seat. When I eventually hear Sarah at the window I pop out of the covers immediately. She wants me to go to the hotel that Chris paid for. He's waiting outside my car too, brimming with apologies. I tell him I'm going up to sleep, and that's it.

Sarah and Chris do drugs, I sleep, and then it's morning. I leave Chris at the hotel, never to be seen again, and drop Sarah off at the Salt Spring Island ferry terminal. I've gotta get out of here! I hit the highway, nose pointed south to the USA border. It's time for some real adventure...maybe Vegas, California, Seattle to start, and Portland to see my old painting assistant. That's it. I've got a plan, a sort of plan, enough of a plan at this point. All I care about currently is my mental health and well being. I'm in search of something: security I think, and a feeling of walking true with the universe. I wanted to listen only to my intuition and act accordingly. So far, it's been a blast!

I reach the border and am asked to step inside the terminal. Leo comes with me and sits politely on a wooden bench. I am greeted by a very handsome border security guard, who begins asking me questions about my reason for visiting the United States. I tell him about my recent breakup and just needing to get away. I tell him about my friend in Portland and my plan to travel a little spontaneously. He mentions that my car is packed pretty full for a road trip, something I hadn't even considered. I'd just bought a box of books on clearance in Kamloops, had nearly every clothing change option available to me, and packed my djembe drum and hula hoops for good measure. The car was stuffed to the tits. You never know what you might need in a pinch. "I'm sorry, but we cannot grant you access to the USA due to your car's capacity and the likely potential of you intending to reside there."

"You think I want to live in the U.S.?! Are you kidding me? I'm from the true North strong and free. Who would ever leave Canada? We've got free health care, Tim Hortons, and the people are actually friendly...not like this bullshit."

He laughs a little at my outburst.

"I'm sorry sir, but you seem very friendly. Are you by chance Canadian? Be honest with me...when you drive to work in the morning, which side of the border do you come from?"

He won't answer, but I continue on.

This time talking to Leo.

"They say America, fuck ya! I say "Fuck you, America." I would never live in you. Never need to travel there anyways. I can see it all in the movies, New York, Vegas, already been to California. I'm not missing out."

The man continues to fill out paperwork and then asks me over to another counter. He passes me off to another guard, who does not have the same welcoming manner. He is curt and to the point. "We're going to need your information. And your fingerprints."

This is when shit gets real. I haven't been fingerprinted since I was twelve and they made us ID badges at school. Well now that I think about it, they likely printed me in the drunk tank….but I was drunk, and don't remember.

"Why do you need my prints?" I demand. My hands start shaking.

"In case you try to enter the United States again, you will be flagged as a potential risk."

I suddenly can't catch my breath. I begin gasping for air. Tears start to well in my eyes. I feel like a criminal. But this time it's not exhilarating. I feel trapped. So excited to hit the road and really be free, I now must turn around and face the drama I've been trying to outrun.

I finally calm myself enough to stand and scan my prints into the border security database…forever flagged as a flight risk. I get back into my Caviar Can, taking one last longing look at the U.S. border, and then hang a right to the off-ramp back to Vancouver.

Maybe some women aren't meant to be tamed. Maybe they just need to run free until they find someone just as wild to run with.

-Carrie Bradshaw (Sex and the City)

Jun. 10, 2018 · 🌐

SLIM

RIOT

Now I don't remember exactly when I started carrying Slim, my blue steel crowbar, but the feeling of a cold metal thumping stick at my side made me feel much more confident in all my adventures. I'd actually gotten Slim as a jewellery-making tool when I lived on the Sunshine Coast, and simply carried it around from house to house, unaware of its greater potential. It was a pry bar on one end, and the other end was tapered so I could use it for pounding out rings. The guy at the shop offered to cut the tool in half, and hence Slim was born, named after one of my favourite rap artists Eminem, or Slim Shady. At this point, I carried my stick with me almost everywhere. When it wasn't in my purse, I had it tucked neatly between the handlebars of my motorbike, beside me in the car, or lying coolly between my thighs. I became a more aggressive driver when Slim was around and a more aggressive human in general.

On this particular night I was wearing the same power cocktail dress I'd been wearing under my blue robe the day before with Chris (at least I think it was the day before): roses atop black stretch lycra, barely reaching the middle of my thighs, and hugging my ass so perfectly. I was wearing my power heels too: black wedge boots that I can really stomp around in—the perfect riot gear. Unfortunately, this skin-tight number left nowhere to hide Slim. I park the car, tuck my blue stick into the crease in my seat, give Leo a gentle squeeze, and set out on another night's adventures. It's not long before I've met friends in the parking lot. Chatting away with a chauffeur in a bowtie, I suddenly hear screams from the alleyway. "Ooooohhh. Drama. Let's see what's going on," I announce as I take off in my platform wedge heels, most people more inclined to head the opposite direction.

The alley's dark, but I can see a shadowy figure sitting by the dumpster motionless. I walk closer and a tall man on the other side of the steel can comes into focus. Then another shrill scream. I see the tall man's hand raise and that's when I notice the top of a woman's head. He's beating her! This is really happening! Still the other figure does nothing but sit silently. It's not his business. It's called street code. Snitches get stitches style. Although I've been living as a vigilante vagrant for the past few weeks I'm still not ruled by this code of silence bred with fear. I refuse it. I am a Riot. I was born to break the rules. "I'm calling the cops!" I scream. Again,

"I'm calling the cops, motherfucker!" It takes four more bellows until the man stops beating her and turns. "Put the phone down, you dumb bitch," he snarls and starts walking toward me. I glance backward and notice that not only the bow-tied chauffeur, but two bouncers from the Granville Strip nightclub have got my back as well. I don't know where I am, so I throw my cellphone at one of the bouncers so he can direct the police. Then, with all of the rage that's been building and all the energy I've been experiencing I lash out at the evil man. "Walk it!" I scream "Walk it! Walk it! Walk it, motherfucker! I've got a crowbar in my car, you asshole and I will scrape your face across this motherfucking pavement!"

I'm a little shocked at my confidence.

He hurls a few more insults and then takes off down the alley, my bouncer friend giving the police the address, and the woman he just assaulted trailing behind him. I can't believe it! I holler after her, "You might not want to follow him. He kinda seems like an asshole." She stops and debates, and then is gone after him like a flash. "Probably a drug dealer," one of the bouncers scoffs, as if he sees this night after night.

Our little crowd dissipates quickly and I'm left standing and shaking in the dark alley alone. I manage my way to a wall and lean my back against it. My whole body collapses to the ground, my platform heels shooting out in front of me into the mud. I grab a couple of nearby rocks, palming them, shaking, as I debate what I'd do if he came back. My heartbeat quickens. I can hear the sirens in the distance. My breath escapes my body as if it had been trapped; heavy convulsions take hold of my chest and I suddenly begin to pant violently, barely able to catch the now tepid air around me. I have asthma, but I've never experienced an attack like this one. I sit for what feels like an eternity, grasping hold of what bits of oxygen I can.

Finally I am able to stand.

I tug my dress down over my ass and brush off what bits of mud I can from my black suede heels. I begin walking past the dumpster where I'd just saved another human being's life and begin to well with emotion. It's like nothing I've ever felt before. I feel invincible and all powerful, like a warrior sent to do good for the earth. My emotion is uncontainable and I let out a deep guttural war-cry, beating my chest as if I were an alpha gorilla in the wild. A couple of figures shift in the darkness, trying to avoid my sight. I don't care about them. I bellow again, everything inside me pouring out and echoing off the graffiti-laden cement walls.

And then it's silent.

I didn't know it could be more silent.

"If you have enemies, good that means you stood up for something."

— **Eminem**

RANDY

RIOT

After the dumpster incident I am thoroughly shaken. Everyone becomes a potential attacker. I carry heavy rocks, knives, Slim, and other homemade weapons in my car. But most of all, I carry a heavy chip on my shoulder. I am aggravated by everyone. I jump at the slightest noise. I drive like a maniac. Yet I also keep notes about shitty drivers on tiny scraps of paper around my Caviar Can. I quickly scrawl license plate numbers, often yelling, swerving, braking...all with the intentions of later calling the police on the other drivers. Seriously, someone cuts me off - writing down their plate. Someone blows by me at forty kilometres over – writing down their plate. Hell, someone blows by me with too much smoke from their exhaust – I'm writing down their plate. I am the epitome of on edge. I even get a warning call from a constable one day after shaking Slim out the window at some guy who apparently had kids in the car. I told him I merely flipped the guy the bird. He still wasn't impressed. It wasn't good.

It's time for a break. A break before I break. (If I'm not yet broken that is.)

At this point I've been fired from my painting gig, quit my government job, and now need to ask my pub manager for stress leave. Yes, you read it right. Three jobs! And I was balancing them nicely. That is until I became the only painting instructor in town, teaching at least three times a week, sitting behind a government office desk all day and slinging drinks all night...everything slowly fell apart. I needed to get away! The Okanagan felt full of old ghosts and new enemies. There was literally forest fires blazing everywhere around me and I just couldn't handle the heat. So once again I head to the highway with my little dog Leo and our shiny red Caviar Can. I barely make it through the pass to Kelowna, flames licking up the forest on either side of the highway while massive water tankers bomb right next to the car. Somehow the universe works in my favour, and I'm free.

I'm finally free!

I've got $10,000 in the bank, sturdy tread on all four tires, and a car packed with all the things I could need for any sort of escapade.

Four hours later and I am crossing the Lions Gate Bridge, my heartbeat quickening as the promise of adventure fills my veins. The tall steel bars of the bridge pass by quickly, and I turn my head side to side rapidly, trying to catch glimpses of the ocean harbour down below. Theo never wanted to live by the ocean again, whereas I felt eternally drawn to it.

First stop: find some WIFI and coffee. My go to in any new city: McDonalds. I take the first exit I see to East Vancouver, an area I've grown to love.

Fourteen years ago I was fourteen and visiting East Hastings for the first time. I wanted to save the world: so many homeless and hurting, all locked into a few block radius. It always seemed like homelessness was a disease here, an airborne illness that Vancouver's rich chose to quarantine to the East side. Since my adventures in 2004 these people have felt like my people. I couldn't feed everyone soup or clean enough bunks for them all to sleep; I couldn't change the system entirely, but I could make a difference one conversation at a time.

I pull into the parking lot of McDonalds by the SkyTrain on Commercial and Broadway, one of the only places I know how to get to in Vancouver, and drive myself around back to park. I'm thinking I'll watch a movie on my laptop, using the

McDonald's WIFI. But as I drive around back everything changes. A homeless camp is set up, numerous people with bags of clothes line the walkway to the SkyTrain. I park and hesitantly get out, worried I've entered the ganglands. I quickly notice, however, that the people have blankets out, lined with their goods and they're selling to the crowds walking to the SkyTrain. It's an impromptu flea market. I love flea markets!

I wander in and immediately make friends with a girl selling ladies clothing. We chat about life and how she came to be at the market. Apparently all the clothes they sell come from donation bins they break into around the city. I remember hearing a story about a lady getting trapped and dying in one, in fact: risky business. It's different people every day and different setups. No regulations, just bartering for a day's wage, that's it. I'm intrigued. And I want in.

I notice a tall lanky guy join the group and begin selling things off of his buddy's mat. He's wearing an eclectic variety of clothing to say the least, and a tarnished chain-metal looking necklace dangles long below his scruffy beard. I notice immediately that he doesn't just sit idly by, as most do, hoping the city dwellers notice his goods. He's up in their face, picking out particular items he thinks they might like. He offers styling tips and colour combinations, a necklace to go with that skirt, etc. Having worked in sales all my life, I love his tenacity. We begin chatting, and a flirt is in the air. His name is Randy.

I hang around for hours watching people come and go, a buzz of sky-train traffic constantly walking through our market. The sellers come and go also, needing to replenish their goods. I know its main vein is theft, and the spoils are drugs, but I can't help falling in love with this tiny market.

I walk toward the sky-train to find a place to smoke. Standing there all alone, also smoking, is an incredibly handsome man with a hard hat and muscles bulging out of his high-vis vest. Honestly, I can't remember what he looked like, just that I'd never met someone so handsome. With no hesitation, I introduce myself to him. Yet another Randy—go figure—and I'm immediately smitten! He doesn't talk much…but he doesn't have to. There's an aura of power and raw unspoken sexuality that radiates from him. We finish our cigarettes and I tell him I'll see him on his next coffee break.

Two Randys and now this girl is randy as fuck.

He heads back to work and I walk to my car in the tiny crowded parking lot, pop my hatchback, empty a few milk crates from my back seat, and lay them out in my new *living room*. I'm claiming this space, this parking lot. I like the ambiance. And I think this market could be so much more. I plan it all in my mind as I unpack. I can buy a coffee a day from McDonalds as pad rent, and invite anyone I like into my dwelling. It will be a safe haven for the needy, an area to commune and share and support. It's not long and I've got a whole house mapped out in my mind. The people that want to do drugs are sent to *the kitchen*, a private area butting up against the sky-train station where Randy and I first shared smokes. The crows get the back forty by the dumpsters, and then of course there's the *living room* with milk crate couches, where everyone is welcome. Apparently no one sleeps in Riot's house, because I never mapped out bedrooms. But I did meet the building manager, for real, and we talked about my grand ideas for the market. "Draw me some plans" he told me, and I set to work. "Riot's Lane." That's what I was going to call the market. Paint flowers and swirls on the sidewalk, bleach the walls, ditch the graffiti. The people would come. And the homeless would benefit.

I wait around for the first Randy to finish selling, offering to buy us beers and hit up a beach. At first I find his enthusiasm contagious. But as I wait I begin to get more irritated. Most of the sellers have left, and the market begins to quiet down. Somehow Randy has accumulated an entire cart of prime goods, Prada loafers and such, from another seller for twenty dollars and he's refusing to leave it anywhere. And me, fresh on the hunt for adventure, agrees to forget the beach.

While he packs up his overstuffed cart I go for a little walk with Leo around the block. We come to a business front and go to have a seat on the speckled pavement steps. Suddenly I notice a drug kit, blood, uncapped needles, and I rage! I begin screaming into the streets "I can't be the only one to clean up this shithole. Get down here and clean up your mess before I start a motherfucking riot!" A few more screams and Leo and I continue on our walk. "I'm giving you twenty fucking minutes!" When we circle back I see a figure standing hunched over the needles and blood.

He's cleaning it up!

My threats worked!

I get closer and see that this is no ordinary man. This is Eddie Vedder, lead singer of Pearl Jam and creator of the most amazing soundtrack for the movie "Into the Wild". (I had recently found out that Eddie Vedder sang for Pearl Jam, and had been blasting their music for the past week or two. To this day I can't tell you what Eddie Vedder looks like, but I was certain this man cleaning up the blood kit was him). I'm gobsmacked.

"Are you Eddie Vedder?"

He's wearing a long dark trench coat. And, even though it's night, I know it's him. I've heard rumours that he lives on the East Side. And now I know they're true. "Uh, yeah, yeah I am,"

"Oh my god, your music has been saving my life lately. That song 'Alive'. Jesus Christ! I've got these friends...well they're not really friends. And I've been sent on a mission, to do just what you're doing actually. You see we all have to play a part. And now you're doing it. You're really here!"

I can tell my enthusiasm is freaking him out a little bit, and he jumps back when I go to touch his arm.

"Just let me clean this shit up, man. That's what you wanted, right?"

I thank Eddie for his good work. I'm acting so erratically, he probably thinks the kit is mine. I continue on my way back towards the seller Randy. He's trying to find a cab big enough to fit his cart full of goods into. After so much back and forth, we finally decide to ditch the cab idea and instead head to a nearby park to sleep.

I follow him slowly in my car, lighting up the dark street in front of him as he pushes his heaped-up shopping cart a few blocks from my *living room*. I park next to a beautiful old building and begin unloading my car to make sleeping room for us both. For some reason he doesn't want to leave his cart outside the car, so instead pushes it a block down into the park to stash it in the bushes. When he returns we snuggle in for some sleep: Randy, Leo, and I. He tries to make a move, but I shut him down instantly. I need affection and human touch, but I'm not ready for sex or any sort of deep intimacy.

In the morning he's eager to go make money, and I'm eager to be on my way. Over the evening we'd developed a sort of animosity, each of us wanting something different from the other. Randy leaves for his cart and I begin unpacking and repacking my car...again. The beautiful building I've parked next to is a school, and it appears that a summer camp is in session. I notice some kids watching me from the bushes, and an old Asian man across the street continuously coming onto his front porch and staring. My senses have been heightened lately. Nothing goes unnoticed, especially the feeling of eyes on me.

Soon enough the 5-0 roll by and ask my name. They tell me I've got one hour to pack up and move along. I scoff a little under my breath and continue packing at the pace I'd begun. *I'm not hurting anyone*, I think. *Am I?*

I head back to my *living room* and stay there for days, maybe weeks, I can't remember. I see the construction worker Randy often and we flirt. Even though he remains professional, I know he wants me. I only see the seller Randy one more time with a cart heaped full, peddling in the hot sun, down Broadway. Good riddance. I mean, it's not like he's done anything wrong, but it doesn't take much to make me angry these days. I spit out the car window as I pass him and hurl a couple insults.

Later that day, I decide to put out my own displays amongst the sellers; nothing for sale, just objects I love, things that represent me. It's like I want my new community to see me for who I really am. I'm not an imposter. I'm here to help. I renovate the *kitchen* into a homeless shelter, laying out an old stained sleeping mat I got from a man in Nanaimo, a first aid kit from my car, leaflets from local businesses, and free papers I grab daily from around the block. My shelter sees all sorts of clients; clients who become friends.

I can remember Spirit, Merlin, Diane, and Tony, and so many more who remain nameless in my mind, though their faces distinct in my memory. I remember Spirit was suicidal. He needed heroin. I gave him money. Merlin was a kid who ran away from home and was one of the salesmen at the market, coming daily to peddle goods. Diane had recently been beaten up by her boyfriend and robbed of her last $40. I gave her $40 from my wallet, and she gave me a beautiful pink butane lighter....the kind you smoke crack with. I offered to burn her boyfriend's eyes out with it for hitting her, but she was much more about peace 'n love and all that. She was clearly terrified of him. Then there was Tony, one of my first friends to visit my *living room*. Him, Diane, and I sat solemnly the night she told her story. Tony, not a user himself, but a long-time witness, taught Diane to turn her glass pipe as she smoked it to get a more even burn from the bulbous glass bowl.

He was there the day I took in two Cherokee teenagers, offering them each an apple and a seat in my *living room*. I can't honestly remember what band Tony was from, but I know the two boys wouldn't look him in the eye. It was a matter of respect. Surprisingly however, they sat together in ***my*** *living room*. Not speaking, but sharing space – peacefully. That in its essence was everything I was aiming for in my happy little riot, peace and equality for the people.

"It isn't enough to talk about peace. One must believe in it. And it isn't enough to believe in it. One must work at it."

-Eleanor Roosevelt

my livingroom.

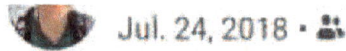 Jul. 24, 2018

Soooo many people I've met lately tell me respect is their #1...yet dont recognize how their words dont match their actions

Respect is #1 ALWAYS!

You will have mine until the moment you prove you dont deserve it. And often it's those people, most would never consider trusting, that keep my respect undoubtedly.

The rough people are the ones whove been through shit, had to prove their worth, save lives, maybe even take some to protect and respect the people around them

I have so much love/gratitude/respect for the people not working the 9 to 5, but still walking this earth with their heads held high

If we're not here to help one another...wtf we doing??

Riot on my loves

PEOPLE ARE NOT ADDICTED TO DRUGS AND ALCOHOL

Artist - Norman Duenas

@_AWAKEN_ONE_

THEY ARE ADDICTED TO ESCAPING REALITY

The Madman and Stoner Joe

RIOT

I pull into the PNE parking lot and make my way to a quiet spot at the far end away from all the other vehicles. I crack another Grapefruit Palm Bay, chucking the empty one into the back seat, and dig my phone out to call my mom. It's been a while since I've talked to her. I used to love hearing her voice everyday. Made me feel safe amidst the chaos. But lately, everything has been so dramatic and feels like it's falling apart. And I don't want to drag her into my bullshit.

Today however I am in good spirits. I've left my living room and my friends and been driving all around Vancouver, purely to learn the lay of the land.

I sit, watching the rollercoasters roll and plumet over and over, rehearsing what I'll say to my mom. I want to talk to her. But I don't want her to worry. I don't know if she'll understand my mission. I don't know if she'll approve. I've been off work for a couple months, voluntarily living with the homeless in the streets...it's every mother's dream for her offspring.

Now, as with so many conversations during this time, I can't remember exactly what we talked about, but I know we chatted for hours. Sipping my booze, sitting on the ground, resting against the car, and soaking up the sunshine. It felt so good to be away from my *living room*, away from the police, away from my street friends, escaping purely to chat with my Mama Bear. I didn't know it would be the last time I spoke with my mother. If I had, maybe I would have paid more attention.

From my mother's memory

"In August we had one of the best conversations in a long time. Our chats were normally hours long with her talking the entire time...no breaks. One endless sentence. This last conversation, August 5th, she stopped and asked me how I was! This was new and gave me hope.

That was the last day I heard from her. She didn't text, she didn't call, I was terrified her rage had finally gotten her dead and thrown into a dumpster. I waited five days then called in a missing person's report."

We finish our chat and I start up the car. Blasting from the radio is news about it being gay pride weekend in Vancouver and I'm ecstatic. I haven't been to a gay pride festival since I was 18 and stumbled upon one in Montreal. And this is definitely an affirmation of my ever-growing belief that the universe (or God) will put you where you need to be and when - if only you take the time to listen. I beat out a few beats on my djembe drum, finish my drink, chuck the can in the back, and head towards downtown.

I drive for what feels like forever through the Vancouver streets scoping out parking, which is futile at this point as the festivities have already begun. There are shrouds of people everywhere! I feel such a sense of urgency to join in the rainbow clad crowd. In today's day and age, we call this F.O.M.O., better known as Fear Of Missing Out...and I've got it bad! I pass by a big stage with people dancing and loud music filling the streets. I want to party!

But where the hell am I supposed to park?

Finally, I find an alleyway with a spot I can just squeeze into. I don't think it was a legal parking spot. But I also don't think I cared. I start my usual routine of unloading the car, bags everywhere, piles of clothes on the roof, makeup kit out...this shit's getting serious. I crank the stereo in the car and begin to orchestrate the tackiest rainbow outfit I can find. Mismatched bangle earring, an ultra tight Hawaiian flowered dress, knee high socks, and an 80's looking high ponytail. I drink while I dress (switching to smores flavored vodka now) music thumping, treating the entire alley like my personal walk-in closet.

I notice a man at the far end of the alley peeking into trash bins, and I immediately think of the silk lined leather jacket Mike had left in my car...a story I'll tell ya a little later.

"Excuse me. I've got a really nice jacket I no longer need. I think you might like it?"

The man comes closer.

And, being totally receptive to any adventure put before me, I offer him a sip from my flask.

I open the hatchback and perch myself on the bumper, handing him my flask again.

His swigs some back with delight, a large toothless grin beaming from his scraggly beard.

The urgency to leave for the pride parade is subsiding. I'm realizing that I can bring the party anywhere I want. And right now I want to party with this old crusty man in this alleyway.

Don't ask me why.

I just do.

Maybe it's because he reminds me so much of my dad: similar build, similar beard, similar gruffness with an underlying sweet heart. We hang out for a couple of hours just shooting the shit, playing tunes, and getting tipsy.

Now I should probably set the scene:

The alley is dark. It's probably 8 or 9pm. No one is in sight...at least that I know of.

I'm a young 28 year old woman - scantily clad in rainbow attire - choosing to hangout with what appears to be a homeless man - likely in his 60's but looking older and rougher - also with nothing better to do.

At some point we end up talking about prison and the Madman relays one of his favorite stories from behind bars.

"I get put up in the cell with a big motherfucking dude. Fat fuck. Once the guards leave he immediately corners me and begins to unzip his pants"

At this point the Madman is basically dancing around the alley, tipsy from the vodka and thrilled to tell his tale. He jumps side to side, mimicking the dance of him and the other inmate, until suddenly he comes storming towards me, our noses nearly touching, the smell of smores wafting heavily from between his rotting teeth.

"I looked him dead in the eye, grabbed his balls in my fist, and told him 'I'll rip em right the fuck off you motherfucker if you ever try to corner me again'"

His voice is more like a growl, and the sporadic enthusiastic happily dancing man has left a much more angry and anxious soul in its place.

He stares me straight, still nose to nose. And I am not afraid.

Suddenly, he jumps back, grabbing the flask from my hand and takes a big swig, then continues dancing jauntily around the alley.

Suddenly out of nowhere he announces,

"I've got a present for you!"

And he takes off.

He's gone for a few minutes, until I hear rustling and a sharp scraping sound from up the alley. Dragging with him, the Madman brings out half of a sparkly red drumkit. Two drums, and one frame, all in my favorite colour...I am overwhelmed and so excited! I used to play the drums as a kid and always wanted a sparkly red set.

I immediately set to making room in the Caviar Can to shove them in; but things are getting a bit squishy.

After a bit longer at the car, I manage to squish it all in the back, when suddenly something catches my eye moving up the alley. Something dark scurries in the distance. I begin to stalk it, slightly drunk and overly excited about the creature. Its movements are too erratic for a house cat, and it's too big to be a squirrel. A little closer, and I realize it's a skunk! I play with it a little, teasing it onward in its stroll, and then decide to turn back to the car before I get sprayed. (Hell, thinking about it now, had I been sprayed I'd have to have bought tomato juice and taken it to the ocean to bathe with; that would've been a funny sight.)

Upon wandering back I see the Madman standing next to my car, with someone I've never seen before. He looks a little rough too, but I offer him a swig of the smores vodka. Apparently he's been sleeping in the SUV parked down the alley and heard our fun and wanted to join. He declines a sip of vodka and instead rolls us up a joint.

"I'm Stoner Joe" he chimes in, rolling the crystally green bud into a zigzag rollie paper.

I giggle at his nickname, but hell, with a name like Riot, I'm certainly not one to judge.

He lights up the joint and the party really begins.

Flask nearly dry I suggest we all go downtown to find some fun and another drink.

A couple puffs more and they both seem down for the adventure.

I check my makeup, tug my little Hawaiian flowered dress further down my nearly exposed ass, and make sure I've got everything I need for a night out. Lastly, I decide to snap a photo of the tall buildings surrounding me, having no real clue where I am and no idea how to set a pin on my phone. As I've said, I hold little faith in my sense of direction after leaving Theo. But I'm hoping a couple mental images and a couple snaps on my camera phone will help jog my intoxicated memory later tonight.

I hadn't yet noticed how beautiful the building next door is; a tall stone structure with dimpled bricks and rich green vines and mosses growing up the walls. I snap a mental picture before wrangling up the boys and setting off on our night's adventures.

So, the Madman, Stoner Joe, and I set off for downtown. But it doesn't take long for them to piss me off and we've parted ways. They want to make a plan, I just want to party and be spontaneous. And as with anything slowing me down these days, I lose em.

And that's that.

I wind up wandering the overcrowded streets. I help a man without shoes get a fork from Dennys. I hit on the sexy black man standing outside of Dennys. Finally, I wind up at a gay nightclub with only an hour or so till closing. I grab a beer and head upstairs to the pool tables, memories of Chris flooding my brain with the gentle clunking of the colourful balls. I remember a cute guy catching my attention, playing pool with his buddy. I start hitting on him, until finally cracking his *friend*, who tells me that the cute one's with him for the night and I can try again tomorrow. It's gay pride. I should have known. I've honestly never cock-blocked a gay dude...I thought it was pretty funny.

I head downstairs to the dance floor, swinging on the stripper pole a few times and feeling so free to just tear it up. And then it's time to leave. But my beer isn't done. And the bouncers are getting angsty.

I hate chugging beer, almost as much as I hate I wasting beer.

The bouncers demand we leave. I put my beer down. But then another guy refuses to leave until his is done, and I choose to do the same. The bouncer begins to get mouthy and handsy, trying to usher us out the door. I remember he was pleading for me to let him go home and enjoy pride for himself. I didn't care. I wanted the beer I'd paid for. (Thinking back now I never actually paid for it. Someone gifted it to me as they left the club a couple minutes back. *A free drink from a stranger? Why the hell not?* Yes, I was at the height of intelligent thought processing at this point.) The bouncer and I get into a verbal argument, which I continued out into the street, even going so far as to call the police on him.

And then I'm bored.

And the controversy isn't worth pursuing.

I begin wandering the streets aimlessly, starting a collection of pride paraphernalia. It's everywhere, and I think about how I'll decorate my *living room* with it when I get *home.* Old posters, mangled rainbow flags, beaded necklaces, the works! During my wandering, I find another random handsome man in the streets and invite him back to the Caviar Can to cuddle.

He agrees.

Now to be honest, I haven't been paying any attention to where I am or where I've been going. Yet, unlike a couple months ago when I was flooded with fear, I am nothing but excited at the challenge of finding my car. I pull out my phone, take one look at the photo I'd taken of the buildings surrounding the alleyway, remembering the brick wall of moss and vines, and lead us onward. Right here. Left there. Up this alley. Down that street. And then there it is, I'm certain of it. One more block and I see the beautiful red brick building covered in foliage.

I feel home.

Up the dark alley, past Stoner Joe's rusted out navy SUV, and we arrive at the Caviar Can.

It must be 4am.

Neither him nor the Madman are in sight.

I quickly start unloading the front seat so me and this random man I've brought back can sleep. He wants to know if I'll drive him home, but I'm drunk and tired, so I say no. He then asks if I'll give him a blowjob, and I say no. We rest for a couple of minutes and then he decides to catch a cab.

Once again, good riddance.

In the morning, a couple hours later, I wake up to beams of dusty sunlight sifting down the alley through the dense

Vancouver fog. I slowly crack my eyes open and see something resting on the hood of my car. Stepping out, I notice Stoner Joe's SUV still parked, him sleeping in the front seat.

I crack the door and notice it's a small bouquet of flowers, in a beautiful glass cup with water and marijuana seeds germinating in the bottom. There's a cute little owl necklace and a note...from Stoner Joe.

It's honestly one of the nicest gifts I've ever been given.

I tuck it neatly into the front seat.

Later that day I return to my living room, begin the usual job of unloading and reloading the car, put the flowers on the cement behind me (still in my *living room*), turn around, and the fucking things are gone!

Like so many things I've lost from this place...gone to theft. But this one hit harder than any others. This was special and meaningful. I cried hard that day. And, while uninterested in any sort of relationship with stoner Joe other than friendship, I treasured the display of affection. It showed me I was making an impact, however small it may have been.

RIOT

GOD

RIOT

The day I met God was like any other. I'd taken to walking around my new neighborhood; East Van always has something or someone to see. On this particular evening my wandering took me under the sky-train bridge, at least ten blocks from my *living room*. I followed some deserted train tracks in, seeing the end of the line leading to a large, locked gate. The acoustics are nice under the bridge, and I could almost hear my thoughts echoing off of the slick grey pavement above me. Almost. Instead, the silence was broken as the sky-train set off and everything around me rumbled, groaned, and roared with its passing.

I glanced around, surprised that I didn't see any graffiti under this overpass. It's then that I noticed a heaped red blanket maybe twenty steps away. It looked like a fort you'd build as a kid out of cushions and your mother's sheets. I walk toward it. "Hello?" I say. God's head pops out from under the heavy red blanket and he gives me a wave. Now I honestly can't remember what He looked like, but I remember clearly how I felt around Him. I was in the presence of someone special. I was safe. That much was clear. We chat a little and He invites me into his home, pulling the red blanket aside and revealing a bicycle with a cart attached to the back. We sit in the powdery dust of His living room and shoot the shit. He offers me a can of pop. I kindly decline; it's obvious this man is hard up. He then pulls out a tiny ball of tinfoil, and begins carefully unrolling and unwrapping its contents. Next, a pipe with more tinfoil inlaid, this piece meticulously punctured. He lays the brown crumbled substance into the punctured tinfoil and passes me a lighter. Again, I kindly decline, and instead watch as God inhales deeply on the pipe. Thick grey smoke trickles from His lips, and His body slumps slightly, His back gently collapsing against the cement abutment behind us.

"I made everything, you know…"

His voice sounds distant, ethereal, as if it were softly falling all around me.

"Including drugs. You don't have to feel afraid."

There's something about His voice, His mannerisms, something familiar. He glances sideways at me and there's a sparkle, just for a moment. I recognize His eyes. He knows I'm onto Him. He's unlike any human I've ever met under a bridge, or anywhere for that matter. I feel a lurking familiarity. He reaches into His cart and pulls out a large orange, rolling its waxy skin from palm to palm. He squeezes it gently and chuckles, before sinking his fingernails deep into its flesh. Then it hits me.

This man is my father!

Or my father's spirit...I'm really not sure.

Officially my father's sixteen hours north of me, but this man....this man is so much like him! And the orange. It's so surreal. I remember my dad telling me about injecting an orange with LSD to bring into a festival when he was younger. And I got the impression that was just the tip of the iceberg to his story telling, though he rarely opened up about much.

God glances over at me again, his blue eye still sparkling between the papery folds of his eyelids. This time however, they are even softer.

They are the eyes of my mother!

It feels like she's right here beside me.

My mother is the antithesis to my father you see; her religious vindication is a sort of ying to his worldly yang. God watches patiently as I connect the dots. His form is still, slightly slumped, yet emitting the most formidable force I've ever encountered. I begin to cry and God holds me. It's all so overwhelming. *What does this make me? Who am I? What's my greater purpose? I'm only a human...aren't I?*

The tears eventually run dry, and all I can do is sit in disbelief and stare. I am full of so many questions. I am full of so many emotions. *Who am I? What am I? Will life ever be the same again?* After what feels like hours of silence God begins to speak. I am compelled to do nothing but listen. He talks with me about Randy, the man in the high-vis vest; about His purpose in my life. It's by no accident that I happened upon the muscular smoke show of a man. "I'm giving Him to you," God says. "May he forever protect and watch over you, my child."

The Earth is silent. We are all that exists in this moment.

I pick up the lighter from God's dusty living room floor, flicking its metal wheel to draw out the flame. The air moves in and around its slick orange glow, causing it to quiver. I pass my fingers through the blaze, again feeling all powerful, as God glances over and giggles. "Go ahead," He says, knowing the desires of my heart. I lift the flame next to an open red umbrella God has propped on His bike, acting as part of the roof for His fort. As the flame gets closer its tip begins to tremor. It touches and immediately pierces the nylon, a large hole singed. I touch it again and again and again, methodically moving my hands until an image appears. A demonic-looking Mickey Mouse face is left behind and God giggles again.

Suddenly a large boom strikes the bridge above us. It sounds like lightning, but heavier. "Can you hear Him? He's with you always. As am I." The bridge shudders again and I shake a little with fear. *Is Randy really up there? He works for the sky-train. He must have access to every station. Did he follow me here? Does He know who I am? Has He truly been chosen by God to be my protector? All I want to do is kiss him...well, maybe more.*

God motions for me to look as a large train, appearing from nowhere, begins chugging down the tracks toward us. "Look," He says, raising His hands and then bringing them together, palm to palm. And the cars begin collapsing into one another, the train growing smaller and smaller the closer it comes. The heavy locked gate to our right slides open as the massive train car—now compressed into one—slinks inside. And then it's silent again. I didn't know it could be more silent.

God and I just sit. I'm amazed. He looks calm and controlled, maybe even a flash of pride upon His face as He shows off to His only daughter.

Another crash from up above and I'm certain the holy trinity is together in this place: me, my Father, and Randy's Holy Spirit constantly looking over me. I have never felt so safe; so loved; so protected.

Now it's difficult to explain if you've never experienced paranoia, but I was certain my story was being watched...by exactly who, I'll never know. But I was definitely being watched. Jesus had the disciples to rehash His story to the masses. And I was certain my new acquaintances, onlookers, seemingly oblivious passersby were likely all wearing wires, and their eyes outfitted with cameras. One glance in my direction and they'd snapped a still frame of my journey, to be shared on some universal timeline I wasn't yet privy to. Hell, if Google glasses are a thing, it'd be ignorant to think no one's watching me and documenting my journey.

So, being the little Riot that I am, I set off to give them a real show. "You want something to see?!" I bellow, as another train takes off above me. "We are all powerful! No one will stand in our way!" I grab a stick from the ground and thrust it into the air, once again a soldier leading my troops into battle. I look around and spot the train x'ing sign and lights posted high in the air with a tall ladder attached; it begged to be climbed. Continuing to rant, I begin to climb the ladder. I feel like an actress in the movie of my life. Everything is surreal. The stick is a magic wand, and a sword and, well, a stick—lets face it. But I am all powerful in this moment. I've just met God, my father, and am finally finding my purpose and calling.

Finally through with playing around, I climb down the ladder and curl up inside the blanket fort propped on top of God's bicycle and carrier. He reaches inside the cart and hands me a sweater, a pair of sweatpants, and some oversized sneakers. He stops and runs His hand across the hoodie's logo, a white mark appearing beneath his fingertips. "You got this, Mama" it says in flowing white cursive. He hands me a wad of bills, and I refuse it, so He tucks it into the hoodie. Lastly, He hands me a ring, laced with the infinity symbol. It's His mark, and I wear it proudly as if it were my family crest, knowing that God will be watching and protecting me always.

Manic episodes, according to the National Institute of Mental Health, have several telltale signs, including feeling euphoric, having more energy than usual, insomnia, speaking fast about several things at once, jumbled thoughts, feeling irritable, and doing risky things you usually wouldn't (like spending a lot of money or having unsafe sex). During manic episodes, you might also experience psychosis or hallucinations. Depressive episodes, on the other hand, include signs like feeling hopeless, having little energy, sleeping too much or too little, eating too much or too little, forgetfulness, and thoughts of death and/or suicide."

RIOT

RIOT

In the morning I leave God sleeping and walk the train tracks in search of a good place to take a shit. It's not easy being homeless, or even just acting homeless as I've been for the past weeks. Things as simple as evacuating one's bowels become an onerous task.

My shoelaces bounce around the gritty pavement, almost dancing, as I walk from under the sky-train overpass, past the train tracks where He'd performed miracles the night before, and out into the open street. I stop at a puddle to rinse off the new yellow-soled Nikes, laces dropping and engorging with the rain water. The shoes are too big, which makes perfect sense as God told me they were Randy's. Same with the sweatpants He gave me. I tug the pants up over my muscular calves and wrap the shoelaces up my ankle, tying them neatly like ballerina flats. I tuck my hand in the pocket of my new hoodie and feel the large papery wad of bills. Then, running my finger over the ring, I remember that He's with me always.

The next few days are a bit of a blur, so bear with me. We'll start in the tunnel, with a memory that's distinct. So far

I've been following different signs around Vancouver, with no real clear direction. I am drawn into a tunnel overpass, hearing the faint sound of music. Immediately upon entering, I feel my spirit lift from my body and swirl within the tunnel around me. An elderly Asian woman smiles as I drop fifty dollars of the money God gave me into her instrument case. Hell, I've got more than enough for myself, and her music is so incredibly moving. Even with a close-up look I don't know what she's playing, but the notes vibrate out and echo melodically down the long tunnel hallway. It's so beautiful I take a seat to enjoy, annoyed at all the people passing by without taking a moment to soak it in. This is the difference between being scheduled and living each moment as per God's plan. Sometimes you encounter beauty that before would go completely unnoticed.

When I leave I begin climbing down the cement steps, my nostrils filling with the scents of rotting seaweed and salty brine. A grin forms on my face. I am at my favourite place: the beach. Big tankers and boats full of shipping cargo, people out walking, and seagulls. I love seagulls. I love all birds, really, having grown up raising parrots, but there's something special about a seagull. It's like a reminder I'm at my favourite place. On this particular day I found the biggest seagull I've ever seen in my life...or better yet He found me. It was obvious this was no ordinary gull, not just by His size but by His stature. He looked wise. And He walked with such confidence. I knew I was meant to follow Him. He padded along, a couple feet in front of me, down the beach for a few blocks until we came to a couple of industrial buildings, when He then took off flying. I inspected the outside of the buildings, the red brick cracked in places and paint on the signs chipped and flaking. They looked abandoned. For some reason I felt inclined to climb the dumpster that was butted against the building and perch myself on a little stoop all my own to take in the ocean air. Out of nowhere the police arrived, wanting me to climb down. I can't honestly remember if I put up a fight, but I know that I left.

It wasn't long after, as I was walking down the beach, that I suddenly got the feeling I was being watched, chased even. I began to run, tucking behind trees in the park, my eyes darting to every possible culprit. Everyone was the enemy. Even the motorbikes put me on edge, unsure of whether it was my angels or demons coming to get me. I managed to get through the park unseen and found a construction site with tall piles of gravel and different pieces of unmanned machinery. I scampered up one of the hills, sliding down the other side in a billow of dust. Frantically looking all around for the eyes I could feel on me, I decided to take cover under some of the machinery. Laying my back onto the dusty rubble, I shimmied my body into the tight space between the machine and the ground. I stayed there for hours, motionless, terrified. I can't recall who I thought was coming for me, but I remember the terror distinctly.

In the evening I came out of hiding, oblivious to my luck that the machinery I'd been hiding under was never turned on. I could've easily been killed. I brushed the dust off of my body as best I could, looked around for any lurkers, and continued walking. I found myself travelling under deserted overpasses and through echoing cement tunnels late through the night. I didn't see another soul. I was no longer afraid. I knew that God was with me.

Once downtown, surrounded by towering spires of glass, I felt a calling to a particular building. Circling it, I found what I was supposed to: my new home. It was a beautiful apartment on the second floor that had the lamp left on so I'd know it was mine. I knew I was meant to come here. God was telling me so. While not physically speaking to me with words, the urges of my heart and the intelligence of my intuition knew that He'd been leading me this entire time. I banged on the front door. The lady at the desk merely looked at me and continued on with her work. It must be past midnight. I screamed at the locked glass door, rattling its slick steel handles. Defeated, I walked away, deciding to take a trip around the block, the wind whipping harshly at my bare skin. I came around again and tried the door a second time. The lady still denied me entry. I didn't know what to do, so I waited. It was freezing. I walked the block again trying to find the best place out of the wind. Coming back around, I noticed lights lining the stairs up to my apartment. I knelt down and cupped my hands tightly around the plexi-glass cover, a warming sensation filling my palms. I sit on the stairs and press my legs against the bulb's dull heat.

I don't remember where I slept that night. I don't remember where my car is. I assumed my dog was in my car, but at that point I wasn't sure of that either. I discovered that the money God gifted me was fake, *sky money*, I call it, so I find myself panhandling outside of Tim Hortons for breakfast the next day. I felt such shame. I didn't remember where my wallet was either, but I do have money, lots of it, actually. An Asian man in a suit handed me five dollars and I began to cry. Tears fell on my dirty hands. I filled my tummy with a toasted bagel and headed on my way, continuing up the hill out of downtown Vancouver and into rows of residential housing.

I remember feeling giddy and purposeful, even though I wandered seemingly without purpose day in and day out. I was in search of my man, Randy, and every adventure before me was crafted by God himself. How exciting was that?! Other than asking for money for breakfast, I felt no fear or embarrassment about my situation, living as so many homeless do—rather, I was delighted that I was finally listening to God's calling. I'd always been taught to work hard, fend for yourself, avoid debt, and never take anything from anybody. I felt broken over the Asian man's five dollar bill. I almost wanted to give it back to him, but I was so hungry. The more I thought about it, the more I realized I needed to be broken. I couldn't be a true instrument of the Lord without becoming completely naked of all reservations. I needed to truly understand how the least fortunate live before I can really do any good. Like Jesus, I needed to be a prophet of the people.

I can remember collecting business cards from food establishments with delicious aromas wafting out the doors in downtown. It was my plan to spread the cards around town to give publicity to the places I liked. One sushi place let me sit down and even gave me miso soup before realizing I had no money. I managed to swipe a full bottle of soya sauce before they kicked me out, later using the salty brine as sustenance when I had no food. A couple of drops and my hunger would be satiated, or at least forgotten. I also remember using the soya sauce as a bit of a perfume to cover up the street scent I'd acquired, stopping along my walk to drip a bit onto my wrists and into my mouth. I felt like I had everything I needed.

I wandered past a building under construction, gazing at the many tools and supplies lying around unattended. I was immediately drawn to a large stack of wooden spools, the kind that electrical cord comes wrapped around. I looked around for eyes on me and, without hesitation or a second thought, lifted the rough scratchy wood and hurled it down the steep hill below me. It caught its rounded edge and flew down the hill. I was delighted. I threw a few more, calling to anyone close by to come join me. They looked at me with awkward sideways glances. Someone probably called the cops. It was so fun, so liberating, living without rules, and acting purely on instinct, not a second thought to the cost of the cars or the possibility of someone walking down below.

I continued a few blocks further until suddenly, glancing over, I was no longer on a Vancouver residential street, but at the entryway to downtown Victoria! I could see the painted dolphin statue, the visitor centre, and if I kept walking that way I knew I'd find the parliament buildings, one of my favourite places on earth. What was going on?! God was playing games with me.

If you've ever seen the movie *The Truman Show*, this would be the moment when Jim Carrey discovers his whole life has been on camera, scripted in a sense, all the characters chosen and outcomes pre-planned. I was witnessing a glitch in the system; two backdrops appearing at once in the film of my life. Soon one of the overhead lights would fall and God would appear from a door in the scenery. *Who is watching?* I wonder. *Has it been entertaining? Best to give them a real show.*

I know God is testing me. He's making me flex my willpower. I dismiss the Victoria mirage, keeping focused on my purpose of finding Randy, and continue pandering up the hill. As I walk further I can hear loud chatter in the distance, maybe a couple blocks away, and I notice groups of young people flocking toward the sound. I tuck in with the crowds and we filter into an alleyway, rising into a parking lot, overlooking a swarm of people. It's a wrestling match with announcers, muscled men in spandex shorts, and ring girls in tiny bikinis. I can see it happening over the fence. I start chatting with people and make a couple friends. Soon enough I'm standing in a couple trucks, drinking a couple beers...and then I really feel like rioting. My first idea is to tip the porta potties, but no one will join me. Instead I begin bending license plates at the corners to make funnels for drinking beer. I'm soaked with the foamy overpour. I get some laughs, say my goodbyes, and continue on around the block.

And then I find it; the place I'm really meant to be (I'm certain this time). The place where I'm going to meet Randy.

Since meeting God a few days ago this has felt like my sole purpose, to find Randy, to find my forever man. Sure, I could head back to my *living room* and wait for His next shift, but something keeps calling me onward in my journey. Like I have to prove something or pass a test to finally show I deserve Him. I turn the corner and find a community centre with a plush leather chair outside. I take a seat in the throne and watch as the weather begins to turn. The winds pick up. The seagulls band together. I nestle deeper into the chair. I run my hands along its smooth arms, feeling a couple of divots that I begin to scratch at. The birds start singing, all in sequence, beckoning the storm to come. I scratch harder. The shiny black overlay peels up under my fingernails and I begin to make patterns and designs in the chair. The anticipation builds with the coming storm. The birds keep calling, telling me God's coming. I expect Him to come from above, not on the clouds like you'd see in a movie, but casually walking on the community centre's roof with His high-vis vest and hard hat as if He were contracted. That sounds romantic as hell. I expected Him for over an hour. He never came. And somehow I'm not upset. I know He's waiting for the perfect timing, the perfect timing for the perfect proposal.

I make my way back to my *living room*, using the various bridges and sky-train overpasses around the city as mental markers of where I am. This was another thing I thought I'd never have after I left Theo: a sense of direction. He was always in charge of our adventures. We'd go wandering, and I never had to worry about retracing my steps. He always knew exactly where we'd come from and exactly where we were going. Somehow, as with so many things, and to my own disbelief, I was surviving without the man—maybe even thriving.

Miraculously, everything was there just as I'd left it, including my pooch, Leo, my car, and some of my street friends. They're all so happy to see me. It truly feels like coming home.

We sit in the market and chat, in no rush to do anything but catch up. Suddenly two squad cars enter the McDonald's parking lot. A few people take off, including myself. At this point, who knows what they've watched me do or what trouble they've seen me cause. I take off to the back forty of my parking lot home where the crows live. There's a caged-in area with a number of dumpsters enclosed. I scurry up to it and squeeze my body in behind the wire caging, my back snugged tightly to the glass sky-train station's wall. My nose is nearly pressed against the dirty metal and I can smell the trash warming in the midday sun. I stand there watching the police scope the parking lot for what feels like a half-hour or more. I notice people stop behind me in the sky-train station, laughing at my clever hiding spot, wedged so tightly I can barely turn to smile at them. Soon enough the cops have taken off and I slowly exit my hidey hole, a handful of my new friends chuckling as I return.

So, let's talk a little bit about my new neighborhood. As I've already said, I'm "paying" pad rent for my car and parking lot *living room* through the occasional snack from McDonalds. But there's also a little sushi shop that goes half price after 4PM and a walk-in clinic with an owner that glares at us every time he comes out to his car...which happens to be parked right beside mine. No one seems to like him, so we pee in front of his back entrance and leave our garbage neatly piled on his windshield after every snack. Across the street there's an AM/PM convenience store and a liquor store that I frequent often, or rather send my boys to frequent. The streets are filled with shops and non-stop Vancouver traffic. It's also filled with homeless people. I meet so many of them on my walks to get daily flyers and newspapers for my impromptu shelter, and most of them I invite back for a snack and a visit.

I can't believe I used to be one of those city dwellers, going about my day with purpose in my steps and some sort of hurry in my heart. Yes, I still pay for my perfect little suite in the Okanagan. Yes, I have a beautiful new car to shelter me from the coastal rain. Yes, I am still a "homed" individual, never fully committing to my cause and joining the homeless. But somehow I feel dissociated from all that. The purpose in my walk is different now. It's not about advancing my career, buying the newest and greatest gizmo, or any of that elitist first-world bullshit. My purpose is the people. And every day, new ones come to me looking for help. But the core characters remain the same.

I've got Merlin who'll make trips on his sweet new BMX bike to get supplies. Spirit usually drops by daily, his demeanour always hollow and defeated. I think he comes for human interaction. Then there's the Japanese ninja, as I remember him, always watching my six (aka my back) and bringing a calm protective energy to the living room space. In fact, he would rarely sit with us, and would rather stand, an ominous force, silent in his presence but formidable in his energy. He rarely spoke. I can't honestly remember how we met, but I know he was sent to protect me.

One night he brought home a white dress for me. I never wear white. But when I put it on I felt luminous and god-like. I felt free from the stains of earthly oppression, and even though my feet and hands were black from my dirty surroundings, I somehow felt cleansed. That same night the cops rolled up again, wanting me to clear my stuff from the parking lot. My boys hopped to it as I sat smoking a cigarette. They made quick work of packing up the many baskets of clothes and art supplies and trinkets that I pulled out every day. The police left, chuckling, and I decided to sleep in my car for the night. It is one of the only nights I can remember sleeping in my car actually. Others were spent under bushes and bridges or next to God by the train tracks. Tonight I feel safer in my metal cage. The ninja opened the door for me to crawl in, having left a space in the back seat, and then began meticulously tucking the last of the things around me. "Lock your door," he told me, "Not everyone's happy with you around here." "What do you mean?" I asked, not believing anyone would have an issue with my helping the homeless. "The dealers are getting pissed."

I thought about that all night. Me, just one little Riot, pissing off dealers in Vancouver's East side! Nothing about this scared me, except when he said they'd likely steal my dog. If anything, his statement solidified the reason for my riot. Keep 'em low and they'll keep coming back was the mantra of the dealer. Give 'em confidence and love and they'll fly free was the purpose of my riot.

One of those dealers showed up one day. Black guy, baggy hoodie, McDonald's McFlurry in hand. I remember he stood there, staring, for a few very uncomfortable minutes, a mere couple feet from my *living room*. "Whatcha got there?" I broke the silence. "Looks real tasty. Is it Oreo?" I ask in a mocking tone, looking for a reaction. Again he said nothing, but just stared. "If you ever wanna come hang out, the living room's always open." I know this is his full-blown intimidation mode, but I'm not scared. My buddy Tony stands up from the milk crate couch, arms crossed, and stares back. The guy scoffs, turns slowly, and saunters back down the street.

One thing I learned from my years steeped in depression was that if you change your surroundings, you change your energy. The energy of the streets around me was bleak. Dirty graffiti-laden walls, sidewalks heaped with trash, and a constant stream of city folk. They'd come and go to the skytrain as quickly as possible so as not to dirty their new white sneakers or dampen their feelings of superiority by lingering too long. As I said earlier, homelessness is like an airborne illness here, something to quarantine and eradicate. I think if they could lose the people altogether, rather than simply change their situations, they would. I, on the other hand, have grown to love these people. Each coming with their own story and circumstance, offering up life lessons you'll never hear in the classroom.

I decided I wanted to change the energy of the streets around me, my new neighborhood. And what better way than through artwork? One positive message can change someone's day, and that person in turn affects others. We are all part of one another's journey.

I grab my wallet and walk next door to the dollar store. There's metal caging on all the windows (makes sense considering the neighborhood we're in). I walk in and am bombarded with ideas. I see gift bags that could be chopped up and used for collages, stickers, and colourful wrapping paper. I begin to fill a basket, not caring what the cost will be. By the end of the aisle the basket is full, so I start another. And then another. I leave them each at the end of the aisles, heaped with bright and shiny goodies. As I enter the snack aisle, I start asking people what their favourite snacks are, telling them to meet me out back of the McDonald's next door for a feast. Some people giggle and point out their favourites, while others give me strange sideways glances. I notice a female worker watching me with agitation. I continue piling things into my basket. She's young and blonde and apparently bold, because she confronts me about my shopping. "I'm going to buy it all," I say. The words are raw and dripping with sass.

I continue on to the cleaning section, loading a fresh bin with scrubbies, bleach, gloves, and anything else I can think of to clean up my living room. I grab enough for all my boys, myself, and the manager of the property, who I'm sure will jump on board to clean up the shithole. As I'm filling my bin with bleach I can feel the manager's eyes on me. The stupid blonde bitch walks over to tattle on me. They stand, talking, watching me shop. The manager, a middle-aged East Indian man, asks what I'm doing, and I explain that I'm simply shopping and I intend to buy all of the items—now totalling six or so baskets. He seems skeptical but allows me to keep going.

I turn around and leave the man standing looking puzzled and unsure of what to do. Then, spotting plastic luau cups and leis and other brightly coloured Hawaiian decor, I charge across the store to inspect the treasures. My eyes go wide. I begin grabbing and filling another basket, completely unsure of what I'll do with all the cheap crap. It made me smile, so I'm sure someone will enjoy it. *Maybe we'll have a luau to celebrate when this riot's over.*

I glance up and am standing right next to a person I recognize. I am in complete shock. I stop in my tracks. I haven't seen anyone I know in at least a month. This face is familiar but one I haven't seen in a very long time.

"Andrea?"

"Oh, heyyyyy," she replies, scanning my face and slowly making the connection.

I used to go to high school with Andrea. She was always a bit edgy and we didn't hang out in the same circles, but we still remembered one another over ten years later. I am so excited to see someone I know and be able to explain the amazing things that have been happening to me. I start telling her about my *living room*. "I'm almost done shopping," I say, "You should meet me behind McDonald's...just say Riot sent you!"

INTERLUDE: I find Andrea on Instagram while writing this book and asked her to write a recollection of meeting me in the dollar store two years prior. This is an excerpt of her take on the encounter:

"We walked into a Dollar Tree on Commercial Drive. It was busy, bright with fluorescent lighting, and not in the most 'child friendly' area. Seeing a lot of homeless and drug-addicted people in this area, I didn't think too much as a girl started talking to me. Her arms were full of...bright fake flowers. Her eyes kept darting around and she was cheerfully animated. It took me longer than it should to realize I knew her. Nothing she said made sense, every word came out like a whirlwind but there were no sentences. Ideas about cleaning up the city, bringing colour to depression to cure it like cancer. I didn't understand, and I didn't recognize the person before me. Who was this, and what had she done with Chelsea[4]? She rambled on, never finishing a thought and dropping items in her overladen arms. And just as she had appeared she was gone, off to add brightness to the masses and spread love from her car. It made me so very sad. I thought she was another mind lost to drugs, spun out in a meth psychosis or the like. I hoped that this wasn't the end of the Red Rider[5] that she wouldn't be another woman living in a tent on East Hastings. I remember leaving the dollar store in a state of melancholy, reflecting on how we are all just one straw away from a collapse."

I notice the blonde Russian twat complaining to the manager again about all the baskets I'm leaving around. I

---

[4] Chelsea is the name my mother gave me at birth.
[5] Red Rider was my first nickname back in university. My first vehicle was my cherry red motorcycle which I of course rode while wearing cherry red matching assless chaps and a leather jacket. This look also got me the title of The Devil, which is ironic considering I currently believe I'm a child sent by God.

decide to confront the situation head on. I walk over. Words are exchanged...the exact details of which I can't remember. But I know it got heated. The Russian demands I put everything back. I demand that they help me carry my baskets to McDonalds as I'll likely double their sales for the day. The manager asks that I leave. "I can't find my hat!" I exclaim. It was the cutest sunhat, woven entirely from paper, and embroidered on the side was "Just chillin" in beautiful black cursive. "Help me look for it and I'll leave," I say to the man and begin wandering through the aisles. He doesn't come to help me. My hat remains MIA to this day.

He comes around again asking me to please leave. I can hear customers in line cursing me, others giggling.

"Get her outta here!"

"We're just trying to do our shopping."

"I'm calling the cops."

That last one gets me.

I decide to ditch the hat and head back to my *living room*. As I walk toward the door I notice a card rack and stop to grab something for Randy.

I'm taking this with me!"

I exclaim, pinning the card to my chest and slamming open the heavy metal caged door. I can hear customers clapping and cheering as I leave and all I can do is giggle at the whole incident. Not only do I start riots...I like to think I am one.

I turn the corner and a big grin takes over my face. There's my car, and Leo snuggled on a dress I'd thrown on the ground for him, my buddies all sitting on my milk crate couches awaiting my return. "Hey boys, I'm a little thirsty...does someone mind doing a water run?" I pull out a number of plastic jugs and water bottles from the back seat of the Caviar Can and my gang grabs them up to fill in McDonalds. I feel like the ringleader. They jump at my command and in turn I take care of them. I'm providing bits of food and water, basic first aid if necessary, but most of all I'm providing a safe space. People are free to be themselves in Riot's *living room*. They're free to be vulnerable in a world where they typically have to be so hard. The streets are a place where you don't see nothin', you don't hear nothin', you don't say shit. You don't rat anyone out or you might wind up dead. Like the man who sat silently beside the dumpster while the scum beat his girlfriend, most of these people have seen some serious shit and bottled a lot of it away. It's only human to want to share, to need to alleviate anxieties and worries about one's safety. To live in the streets is often to live in fear, and to live in fear is to have constant adrenaline coursing through you. That'll wear a person out! Imagine never getting a good night's sleep because your backpack might get stolen, the cement's too hard under your head, or the psycho two blocks down has it out for you. Being homeless isn't as simple as not having a home. It's not having mental or physical security. I like to think I offered these people some sort of security.

While we're on the topic of homelessness and security, I'll include this tangential tale of how I got my stained sleeping mat for my shelter and the silk and leather jacket I offered to the Madman.

At some point during all of these blurry few months I travelled to Nanaimo with my little Leo. As noted earlier, it is often a challenge (a daily one in fact) to clear one's bowels when homeless. So here I am, cruising around Nanaimo without a care in the world when my guts start to grumble. I need to poop. I don't think I can wait until I find a Tim Hortons or other feasible resource. I have to poop now! I'm driving down by the train tracks and suddenly scope out a spot that looks bushy and private. There's a car parked close by, but I figure I can duck behind the bushes and no one should be the wiser. I park, tell Leo I'll be right back, and get out of my car. I look around and don't see a soul, grab up a fistful of napkins, stand up and boom! There's a face right there in the bushes I was about to poop in! "Hi!" he bellows, and I jump. Somehow my guts reverse the process they'd been in the middle of starting and the urge disappears. "Thank God," I murmur under my breath. I look up again and notice how handsome the guy is. Mid-thirties, scruffy face, muscular, little dirty, and grubby looking...but hey, so am I.

"How's it goin?" he asks.

"Oh pretty good you know...how bout yourself? What're you doing back there?"

"Just chillin, having a smoke," I hear giggles.

And a couple more voices. *He's not alone! Oh thank Christ I didn't start shitting back there!*

"Okay if I bring my dog out?"

"Sure! I love dogs."

I clip Leo's leash and he leaps from the car bursting with excitement. He tugs me over closer to the bushes so he can sniff and have a pee. At this point the man has come out into the street and invites me for a smoke. I walk the dusty path in, past the first set of bushes, and am greeted by a couple sitting perched against the fence. The man has a brush that he's scrubbing a bangle piece of jewellery with. "Just found it," he says (likely story), "Gonna pawn it for $60." The woman is going through her purse, meticulously laying everything in a line on the forest floor. There's trash everywhere back here, most of it from them I'm guessing.

I glance over and my handsome bushy friend is holding a tiny glass pipe to his lips. The flame licks out from his neon green BIC and ignites something that billowed a small puff of thick white smoke. He exhales and his body slumps, just as God's had. He opens his eyes and catches me staring.

"Speed," he says. "Doctor says I need it. Mellows me right out."

I watch as they each take a toke from the pipe. I politely decline. and then it's time to leave. The couple are taking off to the pawn shop and I ask buddy if he wants to go on an adventure. For the life of me I can't remember his name, but we'll call him Mike. He laughs and agrees. He's got a beautiful Norco bike (the same brand Theo used to ride) and he decides to ride it while I drive. We agree on hitting up the pawn shop first to check for treasures, then make our way to the beach. I grab us two craft beers and he shows me a neat sculpture by the water that we can sit inside. On the way we find the stained sleeping mat near a bush along with a blanket that we bring to sit on. Similar to a large culvert with vines and greenery growing overtop, the sculpture made the perfect hangout spot for Mike, Leo, and myself. We stayed in there for hours just chatting and swapping stories until our beers were empty. He was really unhappy in Nanaimo and told me all about his shit being stolen and having to start with nothing over and over again. Stories about abuse and fights in the streets, sleeping on park benches midday because it was far too dangerous to sleep at night.

Long story short, I offered to give Mike a ride to Victoria, as I was planning to head that way anyhow. We disassembled his bike, stuffed it in the back of the Caviar Can along with his new stained sleeping mat and hit the open road. We chatted for a while and then let the music take over. Next thing I know all I can hear is his muffled snoring and deep breathing with the heavy rise and fall of his chest. The sleep sounds deep. Almost animalistic. Like a growl. The kind of low murmuring you might hear before a thunder clash. Ominous. And nothing inside of me wanted to wake the beast. A feeling of pride overcame me. This man, so traumatized and programmed to be instinctually mistrusting and guarded felt safe enough to pass the fuck out in the passenger seat of my Caviar Can.

I park us at the pier around 4AM and decide it's my turn to snooze as well. He jostles a bit in his sleep, mumbling every once in a while. But somehow I manage to crash hard for a couple of hours. When I wake he's still there beside me, so I take Leo for a little walk and then try to gently wake him. The calm sleeping giant suddenly turns. He grunts, grumbles, gets out of the car and starts pacing. "Morning," I say cheerily. He doesn't look at me. The pacing continues.

"I need a smoke," he says.

I know he means speed. He starts to become more agitated.

"What would you like to do today?"

I ask, trying to take his mind off the drugs. I think I did the opposite because all of a sudden he turns and takes off up the hill.

"Where are you going?!"

No answer. The blue of his shirt gets smaller and smaller as he climbs the hill and drifts into the distance.

Now I'm pissy. He's left his bike—too big for me, his leather jacket lined with silky fabric—also too big for me, and this nasty-ass stained sleeping mat. I'm so agitated I don't know what to do. I pull the bike out of the back and begin leaving the pieces strewn across the asphalt roundabout at the pier. *He'll come back for it all*, I think, *and I want him to know how uncool it was to leave me high and dry.* I then grab his jacket and other items and pile them up in front of my car. I find a scrap piece of paper and a felt and begin a note. I leave my phone number and a few hashtags at the end. #Riottime #Riotsaves #GonnastartaRiot. As I begin to think about my day, I notice passersby start cleaning up the bike parts I've left blocking the street. I feel bad about leaving his bike there so I wait (this bike is probably worth a few hundred bucks at least) and pack the pieces back into my Caviar Can, along with the dirty mat I'm sure I can make use of. What's left, but an old tattered first aid manual, a keychain flashlight, and some other odd trinkets I leave behind in a pile.

I continue on with my day only to receive a text message later that evening. It's some young guy who found my note to Mike. He thinks it's really nice what I did for him and asks if I want to meet him at a beach an hour away. With no set plans, little idea of where I'm going, and a sense of urgency to seek out adventure, I agree. It's become a bit of a drug in fact: adventure. It's exhilarating, sometimes dangerous, and certainly addictive. It's the only drug I've been high on lately, and I love it. I get to the beach. Get looking for my secret admirer. And then another text. He's been put in the drunk tank...or I've just been scammed. At this point I'm a bit disappointed, but can only laugh at the situation. I'm on the hunt for adventure and I've certainly found it on the island.

Now flash forward to my *living room*. I'm smoking a cigarette, midday, surrounded by passersby tending to their busy schedules. One woman stands out, however, looking lost. I approach her to help. She hands me her phone to help translate her Google maps directions, and lays her couple bags of shopping near my car. As I'm helping her, one of my boys makes a joke and I spike my pack of cigarettes to the ground to make him giggle. Suddenly a punk from the streets (no one I've ever seen in my *living room*) darts behind me and grabs the smokes. "Those are mine!" I holler after him.

"Whatever. You dumb bitch." My face flushes with rage.

"What the fuck did you just call me?!"

He takes off toward the sky-train. I chase him.

"Get back here! Those are mine!"

He's into the station now and jumps into a waiting elevator. I keep screaming at him.

"You're a fucking goof," he spews.

The word making my anger rise. Goof means pedophile in prison slang and is the worst kind of name you can call someone. I've been hearing it all over the streets and, as an English literature graduate, have been appalled at the lack of creativity or intelligent design given to the word. I scoff.

"Why don't you actually call me something hurtful," I retaliate, "like an incredulous little cunt?!"

He throws the cigarettes at my feet as the elevator door

begins to close, likely knowing I would stalk the shit out of him on the next floor. It was only cigarettes, but they were *my* cigarettes. So far I've lost nearly a full carton that I bought to trade with people (the streets are just like prison...a cigarette bill buy you almost anything), my djembe drum, my homemade ceramic rainbow mug, and all the change I'd been collecting for the homeless in it, and the bike Mike left. Lost is the polite term...everything was stolen. These people are scavengers.

I hold my cigarettes with pride as I walk back to the living room, so proud I've gotten them back. It's then that I notice the woman I was helping standing nearby looking thoroughly shaken. "I....I just need my phone," she manages to quake out. I look down at the shiny iPhone I'd mistakenly taken with me. "Oh, sorry, hun!" I apologize and pass it over. She scurries off immediately, leaving her few bags, and all semblance of security she'd barely mustered in Vancouver's East side that day.

During this period I was approached by police more times than I can remember or clearly distinguish. Each and every time I became more distrusting, edgy, and eager for confrontation. I also like to think I became more clever.

On one particular evening I was relaxing in my *living room* when a female officer and her male sidekick rolled up. We saw her so often she became lovingly known as Bitch with a Gun. As with so many nights before, they wanted me to leave the premises and were quite confrontational about it. All I remember is not wanting to leave. Arguing. And when they tried to escort me to my car, I dropped into a squat and screamed, "I gotta take a shit!" Absolutely bewildered, the cop says I got five minutes to go into McDonalds. I Can't remember if I took off or what, but I don't remember going to jail that night.

Another evening, a male officer and what appeared to be two female officers-in-training rolled into my living room. I was chilling on my stained shelter mat smoking a cigarette with a Jimmy Hendrix-looking black dude named Chocolate. Again we were questioned as to the reason for our presence and then asked to leave. Chocolate stood up for me. I can remember the silhouette cast at me in the bright headlights of the cop car. A black figure, arms up, afro high, pleading for my right to stay and explaining all the good I was doing for the people. I remember not wanting to blink, so everyone watching this story play out through my eyes would see the injustice so clearly. Again, I knew my journey was being watched. By who exactly I wasn't sure, but this was a pivotal moment and I wanted it remembered forever. Like the infamous image of the woman standing in front of the tank in Tiananmen Square, this man was standing up for something he believed in…and it was me! The cop cuffed Chocolate and put him in the back of the squad car. I still sat, smoking my cigarette, Leo snuggled up next to me.

The cop comes over and begins questioning me about how I know Chocolate. "It's time for you to go," he says. "I haven't done anything wrong," I announce, "and neither has Chocolate!" "Let me worry about him. It's time for you to go!" At this point I've stood up, cigarette in one hand, and a classic old school Coca Cola mug in the other. I'd bought the mug in my favorite thrift shop on the Sunshine Coast and kept it through my travels. I wave the mug around as I argue with the three of them about my right to stay. Finally I've had enough, and I hold the mug high and throw it to the ground with a loud smash. Leo goes running. "Now you've scared your dog!" the cop yells. "This isn't fucking funny anymore. You've got three minutes to grab your shit and get out of here."

I return in the morning. Buy my McDonalds. And then set to work cleaning up the bits of ceramic Coca Cola shards, thinking I'll likely make them into earrings or something to commemorate the event. I was proud of my brashness, my boldness, my commitment to a purpose. I had always been such a good girl. But sometimes good is boring. And good doesn't necessarily change the world.

As the saying goes, "Well behaved women rarely make history" -Eleanor Rosevelt?

After a couple weeks of adventuring around the city, coming and going to my *living room*, I met a young man overwhelmingly interested in my adventures one day. I tell him about meeting God and my mission to find Randy. His eyes are wide with amazement. He hangs on my every word. "Have you seen Him around working?" I ask. The man's wide eyes soften and he looks from side to side to ensure no one else is listening. "I know who you are," he says, a tiny sparkle as he quickly catches my gaze and looks away. "And I think you know what you need to do…Your Majesty." It's then that I realize this man is an angel sent to guide me toward Randy. I've travelled all over the city in search of Him, managing to find my way back to where we first met. But Randy can't meet me here. This is His place of work, the sky-train station, and while it's home to me, He must maintain an air of professionalism and secrecy about His true identity. I look at the young man who'll barely keep my gaze and thank him for his efforts, telling him we'll reserve the nicest of castles for him in Heaven.

I get into my car and search out the perfect outfit to meet Randy in, something short and tight. "Hurry up!" My angel friend calls from the other side of the parking lot. "He's waiting for you!" My face flushes with excitement. This is the moment-the moment I will truly meet my Mr. Man. I grab Leo from the back seat and toss him out the car door, knowing he'll be safe with my new friends and can keep watch over our living room. I slam the door, back up—Leo's eyes wide with shock as I peel out of the McDonalds' parking lot, leaving him standing alone in the dust and rubble.

As before, I use only my intuition to guide me. (It's funny how humans assume God's will is their intuition, as if we have control over our own destinies...but I digress.) Left here, sharp right there, traffic lights change and cars part to let me through. Everything directs me down a long residential alleyway, and when I reach the end I pull over and park to wait for Randy. I imagine I'll hear His heavy work boots first, before He grabs me up with His thick arms. I sit playing it over and over in my mind, trying to stay calm and look coy. The excitement is uncontainable. I'm basically vibrating in my seat.

An hour passes and I decide to go wandering down the quiet alley to give Randy a chance to surprise me. I've realized from my experience with Theo, that being on the hunt for a proposal can ruin the true magic of it. So I simply wander. I find a new black and white striped long sleeve shirt on top of someone's garbage. *Randy must like stripes*, I think as I pull the soft cotton shirt over my head. Then I find a sticker from one of my favorite breweries on the Sunshine Coast with a little stick left, so I save it for my car's bumper. It's getting hot and I duck in under someone's pop-up garage to hide from the heat. I look over and discover a gift from Randy; a yellow bag filled with clues about our soon to be life together. There are recipes—likely his favorite dishes — garden designs and blueprints for our future house, and info about GERD, a stomach condition I've had for years. I'm impressed at how well this man already knows me. Yet I know nothing about Him. *I better get back*, I think. *He's probably at the car waiting for me.*

As I wander back I notice someone waiting for me, but it's not Randy. There's a police squad car parked beside me and numerous people standing on their balconies watching. Two officers greet me, both pleasant. They say they're from the radio. I've been chosen to come on an adventure, but they need to take my car. I agree and hand over the keys, thoroughly excited for the quest Randy has lined up. The police take me aside and begin their interview, asking me many questions about Leo, my mission, and about Randy, why I'm in town and what my plans are now. They switch off asking questions, each one taking turns to check the radio in the car until the interview is over. They sound excited about what I'm doing and the prospects of cleaning up the streets. They take off in their squad car, a tow truck on its way, and I know that I've done it! I've now got police approval for my happy little riot. All thanks to Randy.

Now on foot, I leave the dusty alley and am immediately drawn to a man in a wheelchair. I approach him and we instantly start chatting. He nods down at a recording device hanging from his chair and puts a finger to his lips. This is an interview too! Thank God I've finally got help broadcasting my message. We talk about the homelessness situation in

Vancouver and he chimes in with the hardships of being disabled and homeless at the same time. He hands me a warm beer and I pop a squat beside him. We chat until our beers are empty and he comments that there may be other people I need to meet. I know this is my cue. I know Randy has done all of this. He never said He'd meet me, but I just knew. We connect like that. And now He's arranged a whole day of interviews to have my message heard. God I love this man, this man I've only met a handful of times. I love Randy! I thank the homeless man for his hospitality and continue out to the main road, again led only by my intuition—or rather by God's calling.

His calling takes me onto a bridge and leads me to a couple people sitting at one of the benches. Glancing down at the girl's brightly coloured sneakers, I notice a few caps from what I can only assume are heroin needles. Then I see the syringes next to them on the bench.

A million years ago (or more like fifteen), when I identified as Christian, I would've believed these people needed saving. I was convinced I had been blessed with not only the knowledge of God's grace, but also the responsibility to share it with others. They needed saving. They weren't going to make it on their own. I would have been the one to tell them the Good Word of God's only son, Jesus Christ who died for their...blah blah blah. I would have converted them...because isn't it obvious they needed it?

But today, things are different. I don't feel better than them. I don't assume I come with some greater knowledge than them. I'm just as dirty. I'm just as lost. And hell, I may not do heroin, but I'm not one to judge. I love my marijuana and craft beer after work. Some people choose meditation, others: TV, video games, sex, the list goes on. We all escape in different ways, it's just a fact.

So, while still cautious of my newfound friends, knowing drugs definitely do alter a person's "normal" habits, I sit down on the bench next to them. I spot a sketch pad in their shopping cart and ask if I can draw something. The girl seems delighted and hands me the book. "You need a pencil?" she starts digging around in the cart. "Naw. I got this." I reach down into one of the reusable cloth shopping bags I've accumulated and rummage around its bottom until *squish*. I've found them. An itty bitty bundle of blackberries I'd picked along the way and have been snacking on for sustenance. I can't remember the last time I ate anything substancial.

Immediately I smear my purple fingers across the sketch pad leaving a large seedy stain. She hands me a pencil, completely enthralled, staring, as if I were creating a masterpiece. In a moment I've drawn a flower overtop the purple, something mimicking an iris, with bits of the off-white sketch paper peeking through. She's amazed. They both are, actually. I grin, finding pleasure in bringing them pleasure. And then I'm gone.

A while later I stop to rest in an abandoned doorway. There are boards over the windows and I can see a pile of mail when I open the metal slot. I feel like it's a good place to stop. And resting my feet feels so damn good.

I prop my back against the peeling paint of the doorframe, and my hands begin to play in the dust beneath me. The dirt snuggles into the cracks of my fingertips, and nestles under my nails. *I never have nails*, I notice. I stop to take a good look at my hands, admiring the little lip of dirty fingernail outstretching my fingertip. *It must be because they're so nasty. I don't even want to chew them.* I find myself immediately thinking of my grandmother. No matter how much disgusting tasting polish she'd lacquer on, I'd chew right through until a ridged ripped edge of nail at the tip of my finger was all that was left. "It's a disgusting habit," she'd say. And it wasn't until years later, after commenting on how nice her fresh manicure looked, did she confess to being a chewer herself. "It's why I get my nails done. Don't feel bad. I used to chew right through the polish too." I felt such relief knowing I wasn't the only one who struggled. Even my grandmother, someone I loved and admired so much, just couldn't resist the urge either.

Thinking about it now, this is the exact reason I'm writing to you. I want to demystify my circumstance. I want others to know they're not alone. I want to confess my embarrassing situation, shed the shame (#shedtheshame) if you will, just like my grandmother did about chewing her nails.

I settle my hands back into the dirt and palm the tiny stones, taking my time to really feel their smoothness. Traffic buzzes by. I feel like the only person in the universe. It's just God and me at this point.

I breathe deeply, taking some time to really notice my senses and my surroundings. *The paint chips in this doorway are fascinating.* There are multiple layers of colour and I find myself pondering the history of the building I've come to rest in. *Sure, it's out of commission now, but what was it before? It's a busy street. Near the water. Awkward parking, but the building looks old. It's probably had multiple lifetime's worth of stories.* I look closer at the peeling paint in front of me and begin picking at the top layer. It flakes off easily, leaving me a latex strip, shiny on one side, dusty and freckled on the other. I peel some more, revealing a deep maroon beneath the modern gray. *I bet this colour was called something cheesy...maybe "icy slate" or "marvelous marble." That'd be a sweet job: naming colours.* The maroon flakes into forest green and that into a cobalt blue. *I could make a cool collage* I think, stuffing the paint chips into one of my reusable bags.

The wind whips into the doorway and grabs up one of the paint chips, flipping it in front of me. I grab it up and study it closely. Multiple layers of colour, deep scratches, folded ridges, areas pocked out and weathered from the years of Vancouver storms. I stare at the piece, turning it round and round, until it hits me. There's a face! It's unmistakable. An emperor in fact. His royalty radiates from the chip. It's just a bust, but his stature is solid and formidable. If I recall, he had a headdress of some sort, something that confirmed he held prestige.

I phoned my mother in a frenzy of excitement. I need her to Google this man. I'm sure his image means something. There's a message there, I just need to decode it. God's trying to guide me. I just need to listen. I explain as much as I can about how the man looked, smoothing the chip's ridged edges in my fingertips as we chat. "I think he's Egyptian. Or middle Eastern. Firm brow. See what you can come up with."

My mother tells me later that she did in fact spend a little time Googling, not wanting to discredit anything I was saying during this time. She said she could barely understand the words I was speaking, as I was talking so fast, let alone what the hell I was trying to talk about. It all was basically gibberish. I think she was holding hope I was going to be okay. So she searched.

The day bleeds into night. I may have met more people, but honestly all of my memories are so fuzzy. I figure I should go check out the free showers at Trout Chris everyone's been telling me about, and I arrive there just as dark hits. There's a big field and flowing lights in the far distance that draw me in like a moth. Forget the shower. (I think it's been weeks since I've had one. What's another day?) I walk across the dark field to a bonfire surrounded by bleachers. Two women are fire dancing with glowing-hot hula hoops. It's completely mesmerizing the way the fire encircles their partially naked bodies. The entrancing music draws me to stay and watch.

Once my eyes have had their fill, I continue walking through the dark toward the sounds of laughter. I find a couple sitting on a bench drinking. They invite me over and offer me a Hey Y'all, so I sit chatting aimlessly until it's empty. I thank them for their hospitality and head onward, closer to the bushes around Trout Lake.

I've learned that even the "pointless" conversations offer purpose. They allow God's timeline to play out. Everything for a reason at just the right moment.

It's here, on the dark bushy path, that I meet Coyote; a surprisingly Caucasian, tall and scrawny, hyper-intellectual man needing his story told. He's concerned about the ocean and the whales. That was somehow connected to politics, which was connected to the CBC. Again, it's all a little blurry. He knows some of the main radio broadcasters and wants me to share our combined story.

Now some of you may find it odd to meet a person like Coyote in the dark woods at night, but I felt it was my calling. Everyone and everything put in my path served a higher purpose and my mission became more resolute the more people I met and the more hardships I heard of.

I return to my living room the next morning and Randy's still nowhere in sight—and neither is my dog Leo. I begin to panic. I've thrown my life to the wind for this man. This man I barely know. Could He really be my saviour, my forever man? I begin walking around the sky-train station, hoping He's working.

He isn't.

I glance toward His tool shed, the one he'd pointed out when I escorted Him around the block one day. "You ain't seen *any* tools yet," He'd commented coyly. It was just enough to let me know He was interested too. When I look today at the beautiful mural-covered door of the tool shed, there's no Randy, but there is another message hanging for me. A caulking gun sits precariously on the metal handle and I immediately understand Randy's humour. Somehow He knows about my ex-boyfriend Trevor, and how I've been inappropriately cocked, and now he's giving me the chance to caulk back. I giggle with delight. Grabbing the gun, I pin it tight to my chest, scurrying across the crowded street. Two police officers pass me on the sidewalk and give me a strange glance, but keep walking. *What should I do with this weapon? What would Randy want me to do with it?* I dash across another busy intersection and head into a back alley. I want to leave an impact, an impression, maybe even make a change. I hold my gun tightly and scan the painted walls around me.

Let's start the riot!

I hold the nozzle close to a red brick wall and pull the trigger until warm gooey white sludge pours from the tip. "R I O T" I spell out...and again and again; over here on a cement meridian, once or twice on a large blue dumpster. I want to be remembered. This is my house, why shouldn't people know it? I spot a large black and white mural of a motorcycle on the side of a chop shop across the street. Yes. "R I O" and my gun runs dry. *Damnet.* I think about ditching it, but I somehow feel safe and protected with the metal gun by my side. I decide to change its purpose. My mission is only to spread love, either from my Caviar Can, or throughout the streets around me. My purpose is to share my love. I grip the gun, wondering how best to use it? A grin forms on my face as I decide this will be my love gun, offering a "pop" for every person I encounter who won't smile. Vancouver is full of people who won't look each other in the eye, and certainly full of people who don't smile.

Next step: change that! In any small way I can.

I leave the busy streets, caulking gun in hand, and finally end up in a residential area (where exactly I don't know). I look over at a dilapidated old house and once again something inside me knows, this is the spot where Randy must be hiding. I grip my empty caulking gun to my chest as if it were an AK-47 and I, a soldier looking for a hostage. Climbing the crumbling steps, I am alert and stealthy for any noises or signs of movement. It smells stale and dank. And except for old boards and rat shit, the house is empty. Once again I am disappointed. I exit down the precarious stairwell and sit to take in my surroundings. The air is crisp, few clouds in the sky. "Where do you want me to go Randy?" I listen to the wind. There are no birds to guide the way.

Across the street I see a large truck piled high with rolled sod. I grin. I know this too is a message. Because of my desire to clean up the streets, we're finally going to cover the roads with grass. People will walk barefoot through the lush greenery. Hell, I've been wandering around Vancouver for days. Who needs a car? I've got a vision for a cleaner, better universe, and I know it's Randy that's helping it come true. He's been sent to see my will be done. He's the muscle, I'm the brains, God's the intuition. The Holy Trinity at work in the modern day world. I beam at the driver who, thankfully, for his sake, smiles back. I hold my gun at ease and continue walking up the block.

I stop beside a house where I find a large bucket filled with water. I am so thirsty. I can't remember the last time I drank something...it was likely that Hey Y'all at Trout Lake. I begin drinking the water from my hands. Once again, it feels like I'm playing a video game. Charging around with my gun to my chest, I now need to power up with rations or I'll lose health. I splash the cool water on the back of my neck and temples, its drips trickling under my t-shirt. It tickles and I giggle a little. I wipe them away and continue walking.

Spotting a convenience store, I decide I want something to eat as well, but the cashier won't accept my sky money from God. He demands I leave. I point my caulking gun at his face and love pop him for good measure. "Pop!" I say, and a few more once he's ushered me outside and locked the door, "Pop! Pop! Pop!" He's definitely not smiling. And there's still people in the store all staring at me strangely. I love pop them all "Pop! Pop! Pop! Pop!" None of them smile. I gotta get out of here before someone calls the cops again. I dart across the six-lane strip of traffic, stopping in the middle to do a barrel roll on the grass and army crawl under a signboard with my gun pinned to my chest like a true soldier.

Infuriated, I decide Randy must be at Bon's Off Broadway, my favorite restaurant in Vancouver, and somehow I know it's close. I can't believe I haven't thought of it yet. But I guess Randy needed all the time He could get to organize His perfect proposal. I know it's going to take my breath away.

And I have no problem waiting. I imagine over and over how it will play out. The further I journey, the clearer my imagining becomes, until it feels like I've nearly got all the dots connected. I want it to remain a surprise, but I can barely contain my excitement. In my mind, Randy must be leader of the Hells Angels...it all makes sense. They've been protecting me all along. I imagine the Harley Davidson He must own, more beautiful and powerful than any machine I've ever seen. I imagine the roar of a million engines, His minions behind Him singing to me through the streets of Vancouver as He comes looking for me. The suspense has been unbearable but if I can wait just a little longer I will be the queen, and He my king.

I spot a large transport truck I know I'm supposed to take the rest of the way. I clamber up the tall steps and knock my gun against the passenger window. The driver's eyes go wide and he shakes his head violently, refusing to let me in. I love "Pop!" him through the window and head to the back. The latch is locked. And my gun is nothing but a caulkless metal frame. Guess I've got to walk it. "Walk it!" I snicker aloud, remembering the incident with Chris a few weeks back, or was it a few days? I really don't know. Still giggling to myself,

I continue across the street, gun waving. *Such a bossy little bitch I am.*

Up hills, down hills. Up more hills. I stop to rest on someone's front porch, reclining back into their wooden rocking chair. I'm so excited to see Randy and be crowned queen. I know He's going to have an amazing motorbike for me, something fit for royalty of the Hells Angels empire. All the gruff old bearded men will bow to me, or better yet rev their engines on cue. The thought of the sound, the power being blasted for me, sends tingles between my thighs and even more giddiness to my step. I am going to be so happy and blessed when I complete this mission and finally find this man. My man. My true Mr. Man.

I know my mother will be there, so I pick a beautiful collection of roses from various gardens along my walk to gift her. It feels like forever since I've seen my mother. I stopped calling when things really started going sideways, at least a month ago. I didn't want to scare her. And I didn't care if she wouldn't approve. I was meant for so much more on this Earth than people expected of me. I was meant to make a difference. Apparently I'm a child of God, so making a difference is right up my alley. Not like they say in the bible where everyone's a child of God, I really am God's child...a female, modern day Jesus if you will. It's been a real trip to let that sink in. But *what about my earthly parents?* I wonder as I walk. I'd seen so much of their spirit and distinct mannerisms within the God I met under the bridge. Could they be one in the same? Has God surrounded me by earthly forms filled with His spirit to watch over me my whole life? Suddenly, I think of my dog, Leo, tears forming in my eyes. I think about the way he stared at me; like he was staring into my soul, speaking to me without words. I used to call him my "wise old man," but now I think he may have been so much more, like a guardian angel. I have so many questions, so many unanswered quandaries...but for now I must trust. For now, I must walk.

I spot Bon's in the distance and my excitement swells. All of a sudden a few Harleys start passing me on the road. The guests are already arriving for the wedding! My heartbeat accelerates. I so want to jump on the back of one, but I know this is my mission alone. I've come this far on my own. I must show my man I am a true warrior woman, fit to be queen of His kingdom. I begin running.

RIOT

I finally reach Bon's Off Broadway, home of the $2.95 breakfast, and instinct tells me to head around back. I climb the first set of stairs I see and begin peeking in windows. One is open. I walk up and am greeted by a pale man sitting in front of his ornate mirror applying makeup to his face. "Have you seen Bon?" I ask through the open window. "Sorry hun, have not." I run out of windows to look through and begin tearing at the lattice work barricading me from the roof. *Where will Randy want to meet me?* I hear voices down below and see a man in an orange cloth apron. This must be Bon[6]. I head down the stairs to greet him.

Now as I said earlier, this whole caulking experience has felt like a video game. I've got a gun, a mission, and now I'm meeting the final Boss, the overlord you must annihilate to win the game. Now I really don't remember what this man looked like. But I can distinctly recall him yelling to me,

"Those roses are from my garden!"

---

[6] While writing this book I revisited Bon's Off Broadway to enjoy a cheap breakfast and photograph the graffiti for this book's cover. I spotted Bon clearing plates, the true Bon, an older Asian man. The man I met initially was definitely not Bon. I still don't know who he was.

Then out of nowhere, as I finish down the last step, he throws his leg up in a spinning high kick at my face, barely giving me time to even hear the swishing sound of his nylon track pants as his leg flew past my ear. Caught completely by surprise, I throw up my hand to block the kick (having fairly fast reflexes) and a firm connection is made, crumpling my right limb completely. I scream out in pain and grab my hand gently, running like a wounded animal to hide in a staircase. No one follows me.

Once I've recovered my breath I take a moment to notice my surroundings. This feels like the pit of hell, pain coursing and throbbing through my fingertips, spiders and their gauzy webs living in every dark crack of the stinky cement stairwell. I start to laugh maniacally. Of course! I'm being initiated into the Hells Angels' family. It's full of hardened criminals, or at least on the surface. Randy's got to know I'm strong enough to run with the big boys. I settle my back uncomfortably into the sharp edge of the stairwell...might as well embrace it, I wince.

Soon enough three officers arrive with a paddy wagon and manage to remove me from the stairs and get me in the back handcuffed. I ask them not to lock the cold metal too tightly to my puffed out flesh. I'm pretty sure it's broken. They close the wagon's door and I feel instantly at peace. There's nothing in the back except a dull red light, casting a calming hue around the tiny interior. Of course, I have to spit on the surveillance camera lens for fun, but all and all I like it back here. I can hear other vehicles passing and feel when we stop at traffic lights. I try to imagine where we are, but nothing is distinct...until I hear the seagulls. And I remember, God is with me always.

The paddy wagon stops and the fluorescent lights come on in the interior. The door slides open and I'm in an outdoor containment unit. Five police officers stand waiting, two at the door to help me out. "I'm just gonna jump down," I say, barely getting the words out of my mouth before they grab me roughly and drag me inside. They collapse my knees and take me to the ground. I scream about watching my hand as they viciously pat me down, but they don't care. They take off my cuffs and lead me into a cell. I crumple to the grey speckled floor and ball up.

Another fucking cell.

This time, the walls are littered with bits of blood and a flurry of words and messages painstakingly carved into the door frame. It's by far the nastiest cell I've been in yet. I rub my hand gently, wincing at the pain. I'm certain it's broken. Hearing Smore muffled voices out front, I sprawl out on my belly to listen under the door. The crack is too small. I stand up and derby check the door. Bang! The hit sends the small window cover swinging open. A young dumb bitch cop comes and swings it closed. I smash it again. Bang! It swings open. There's something that's not quite right about this precinct, but I can't put my finger on it. Everything seems to be duct-taped, hobbled together as if it weren't a real prison at all. Maybe more of a criminal's training ground. I see officers walking down the hallway and begin yelling profanities and slander at them. "You dirty pigs....snort, snort. I'm going to fucking kill you when I get out of here. Rip out your eyeballs, stuff them up my pussy, and take them home to feed my dog" and on, and on until I'm out of energy and slump back in the corner of the cell. I begin reading the walls. There must be a message from Randy, something to keep me sane, a puzzle to figure out. Everything is in God's hands. I know I'm meant to be here. This brings me a little peace.

Now I can't explain exactly what I saw or how I came to form such firm conclusions, but a collection of 666s and names scratched in lineage, along with a blood-splattered roof, and I'm certain this was Theo's father's cell. I mean, he always collected old motorbikes, I'm sure he had some connection to the Hell's Angels. *How many people have been watching my journey? Has this been going on my whole life?* He's scratched the names of my suitors into the door frame, crossing out those that weren't up to snuff. The last name, "Red Rye," is freshly crossed and I know it's for Theo. His favorite drink was rye and ginger ale, and his hair was a lovely strawberry blond. Theo's father is a dentist, a surgeon of the mouth, and I believe the blood-stained roof came from his own self-sacrifice. He wanted his son to have a chance to marry me and carry on the holy lineage, but alas, after 10 years of watching over me, God decided Theo had to go. It was someone else's turn to prove their worth and keep watch over his most treasured possession. Above "Red Rye" in massive black lettering is Randy's name, "Kong." I'm sure it's for Him. All of the clothing God gave me of His was black. I can imagine Randy walking the streets of East Van, arms puffed, knuckles nearly dragging, like the big black beast King

Kong was. God wanted someone stronger than all other humans to look after His baby girl. And it's clear from the list that men have been trying to prove their worth since I was born to this Earth.

It's hours before I piece together the puzzle and a few officers have peeked through the little window in the cell, each one igniting my fury and sending me into screaming obscenities again. In defiance I pull down my pants and squat in the corner, my pee yellow and strong smelling. I finish and decide to mark my house further like a wild animal. Using my pinky finger I trace through the piss and spell out "RIOT." This brings me delight, and must've been the final straw, my final initiation into the Hells Angels family, because the next face I see at the window is a friendly one. It's Coyote, dressed as an officer. "Would you like a clean cell, miss?"

He opens the door and I can hear Native drumming outside the police station. It's happened! The police force has been taken over for good. No more dirty cops like the ones who drug me in here. I knew my people would infiltrate. It was just a matter of waiting. Soon their queen will be released. He opens another cell and leads me inside. "Is there anything else you need?" I politely decline and wait patiently for my people to tie up all the loose ends, settle the politics, and sign the peace treaties. Soon enough Randy and I will be together forever.

A few hours more and I'm released to the streets. The drummers have all left, but I know that something great has happened today. Our judicial system will never be the same again, and I'm to blame. Well me and Coyote, I guess. I feel all powerful. The change I wish to see in the world is the change I am making. The only hurdle is myself. Can I stay in tune with God long enough to know exactly where I'm needed? He's speaking to me from so many directions, through so many people and places, animals and objects. Everything is a sign from God if you watch for it.

In fact, the next sign I encounter is undeniable and I giggle at God's sense of humour. I stroll past tall shiny buildings, seemingly made out of spotless glass, thousands of windows surrounding me...which means even more eyes. People carry bags from department stores, briefcases, to go coffees. They all carry with them a sense of purpose, a direction. I, on the other hand, appear aimless. I walk with nothing, going nowhere. God is my guide I, but an empty vessel.

I pass by a parking lot and am pulled to enter. I can feel the anger rising as I look out at the sea of fancy cars, medals of mediocrity, symbols of lives not lived rather worked. It's such a joke. The shinier the car, the angrier I get. While people are dying in the downtown core, the others are layering on the wax, buffing the hubcaps, spit shining the windshields as if money determines worth. Then at my feet appears a large chunk of cement. Its placement's steeped in purpose. No second thought and I've thrown it through the windshield of a BMW and continued on my way.

I cross the street and another row of cars calls my attention. I notice the numbers painted on the ground as I pass by a handful of stalls. Then without warning the stalls stop, number 69...God makes me giggle. I look up and spot it: the Riot Bus. Shorter than a regular school bus, windows caged in with metal lattice work, exterior beat to shit. I know this is to be my chariot for doing God's work. I just need to find the keys. I check the front tire, the back tire, the windshield's ledge and anywhere else I can imagine someone leaving them. I decide to try and open the door with the use of an antenna from the car beside the Riot Bus. I bend the antenna back and forth, but it won't snap free. Disappointed,

I return to the driver's side window and am greeted by two men. I tell them it's my bus, but I've lost the keys. They laugh to one another and the one man gets on the phone to a locksmith. *Finally, helpful strangers. Thank you Lord.*

When the police arrive—not a locksmith—we all have a laugh over the confusion. But then I'm in handcuffs again, and it doesn't seem so funny.

I sit calmly in what can only be an emergency room, the sound of sirens outside and a whirling hummm of chaos all around me. A large man lays in a stretcher beside me laughing hysterically. I can't help but giggle.

The two officers escorting me stand nearby, one leaning against a piece of medical equipment with bold red numbers on its base. The officer catches my gaze and swipes his hand across the numbers, just as God had done with my hoodie. They disappear instantly. He gives me a wink, and I know he knows who I am. He's been sent to protect me, an angel of sorts in all blue. His gaze is so comforting. A ticker reads out a number and the officers come to my side, ushering me into a room.

The room is small and dark, or at least it feels that way with the seven other people standing in it. A bed lies in the middle of the room. Everyone stands around it. The two officers turn to leave, and I cry out to my angels to rescue me. But they must leave. This part of my journey isn't in their jurisdiction. Reaching out, seven people grab at my body to restrain me and pin me to the bed. I thrash and claw, screaming, trying desperately to defeat their grip. All of a sudden I see a needle and I know I must be still or I will suffer further.

What doesn't kill you gives you a lot of unhealthy coping mechanisms and a really dark sense of humor.

Unknown

wordables.

"Here's to the crazy ones. The misfits. The rebels. The troublemakers. The round pegs in the square holes. The ones who see things differently. They're not fond of rules. And they have no respect for the status quo. You can quote them, disagree with them, glorify or vilify them. About the only thing you can't do is ignore them. Because they change things. They push the human race forward. And while some may see them as the crazy ones, we see genius. Because the people who are crazy enough to think they can change the world, are the ones who do." — **Rob Siltanen**

Dr. Abbott

RIOT

The next parts are even fuzzier than the first. I wake up in a ward. A psychiatric ward. Yes, a psychiatric ward! I guess after reading all of this, it may not seem shocking to you, but it sure shocked the shit out of me. Up until this point I've just been following the Lord's plan, my intuition, whatever you want to call it. I haven't hurt anyone...(I don't think) I haven't tried to hurt myself. I'm not hearing things. I'm not seeing things. Well, duh, I'm hearing and seeing things, but they're not delusions...how could they be? Sure, this is all a little weird to me too. But is it really that strange to be called to a higher purpose; to have a calling?

I'm not crazy!

...am I?

Everyone has their own room: white walls, white furnishings, we eat crackers for snacks. In fact there is virtually unlimited crackers, butter, and instant coffee. I attribute this diet and my new medications to adding a whopping 90 lbs over the next year to my already curvy frame! Acceptance of my *new* body is still something I struggle with to this day. But it has really taught me that bodies are just physical vessels for our souls. I am still an amazingly loving, intelligent, and ambitious woman, just packaged a little more plumply. There is a TV. Sometimes people fight over what to watch. There is also an art room where I spend a lot of my time. I draw, write, collage, do whatever I can think of to keep my hands busy and pass the time. I even make a friend. I don't know why she's in here, but we make art together, and it's nice. We part ways and live out our stay in different parts of St. Paul's Hospital. I see her again at the end of my stay in The Heavens and she looks so much healthier, with colour in her skin and more meat on her bones. She was pushing someone in a wheelchair and there was a sparkle in her eyes which had once looked so dull. We smiled and said hello. There didn't need to be more. Sometimes people come into your life at just the right moment and then are gone in a flash. Sometimes people have no idea the impact they've made in your life or how much their general existence has helped you through a certain period. This nameless girl was one of those people for me, and I was overjoyed to see her well.

I spend a week or so in the Psychiatric Assessment and Stabilization Unit before being transferred to the Acute Behavioural Stabilization Unit. Here I have more privileges. There are computers, board games, classes, and even opportunities to leave the ward! I haven't felt earth beneath my feet for weeks. I'm in downtown Vancouver and I haven't even heard the sound of cars or bustling city streets from my second floor dwelling. All I can do is watch the streets from the window at the very end of the hall, composing stories and backgrounds for the people I see. It keeps me semi-entertained. As I sit, three young men pace the length of the hallway, staring straight, eyes motionless, arms barely swaying. They look robotic. They pay no mind to my presence and even less mind to the time. That must be why they do it I guess; to pass the time.

Then there's the guy who hates being touched. Rodney has wild orange hair and usually wears anime t-shirts. Me, always being a bit of a rebel (a real riot one might say) once brushed his hand to see what would happen. It was like I'd smacked his soul. He never spoke to me again but only offered sideways glares and quietly spiteful comments.

The old Asian lady I bunked with spoke no English. She was only there a week or so, and one night decided to wake me by grabbing and squeezing my toe until I screamed so loud four nurses came running. They apologized, but I never slept quite the same after that. I'd let my guard down, forgetting that the people around me were all struggling with their own mental plights. Nothing was normal anymore.

Then Brandon, the sex addict. Dark-skinned, Latino, nice boots. We made out a few times, always getting split up by hospital staff. "No ABSU babies allowed!" the one nurse told me, chuckling under her breath.

Then there was the nurse named Tony. This man thrived on being domineering and controlling. I remember he would constantly bitch about me falling asleep on the couch watching TV. One night he even threatened to not let me speak to my mother if it was going to keep making me "emotional.".

The first bunk mates when I arrived were nice. A girl from somewhere in Africa who must've weighed 80 lbs and never ate during mealtimes, merely pushed her food from side to side. And Andrea, whose eyes always glimmered mischievously and whose body never stopped bouncing with energy. She told me she had two children and was always spending her money on Lego and crafts she could do in the ward and then presumably send to her kids.

Then there was Mary Beth, a lady in her 70s who had full day passes to do whatever she liked. She would typically go home (a nice quiet house in the suburbs I imagined) and work on her gardening, bake marijuana edibles, and God knows what else. I was always envious of the missions she had, so much to do in her time away from the ward. She said she loved it here though, in the ward, and her eyes would sparkle behind her rose-coloured heart-shaped glasses.

I remember one evening running into Mary Beth in the quiet second floor hallway. I'd had to memorize the pathway in, as it was pretty convoluted trying to navigate the hospital; two floors up, left, past the fake money tree, stick to the right, and then down past the old nursing school photos. Then at the very end of the quiet corridor were the heavy double-set doors, locked and monitored via videocam by the nurses inside. Somehow tonight I found my way back, walking past the old nursing school photos...or stumbling rather. I had had the usual marijuana cigarette and craft beer, but for some reason it hit my system hard! Looking back now it may have been the combination with my meds. I felt dizzy and couldn't walk a straight line for the life of me. Thank God Mary Beth happened to appear from nowhere and scooped my arm up and walked me into the ward as if nothing was the matter. The nurses gave us a bit of a sideways glance, but Mary Beth just kept us moving. When we reached one of the quiet TV rooms she sat me down. "Must've been some crazy shit you took." She giggled. A sweet little French giggle. She then told me about all the edibles she'd been baking that day and what new flowers she'd planted.

Many days later I sat down to do some crafting and ended up drawing a large colourful heart on black construction paper with pastels. Mary Beth was in love. She begged me to keep it. She said she would hang it in her house. I like to think that to this day Mary Beth looks at the heart and smiles. I like to think I made a little impact on maybe someone in that ward. I know many of them impacted me.

Then, of course, who could forget John, our resident drag queen and shit disturber, always looking glamorous with his purse and long scarves. Not so alluring was the way John would use the scarves to sop up the long strands of drool spilling endlessly from his ever-moving lips, a common symptom of the medication some of the patients were on. That, and incredibly stinky shits were common for most of the residents, and somehow, miraculously, they all smelled the same. I would watch who received prunes in the morning, guessing they were likely the culprits for the bombed bathrooms, and try to get my morning duties done before them. I also learned quickly not to borrow things from John, or tell him secrets, or really to trust him at all. I think John's battery ran on drama. If he's not in the thick of it, he creates it.

Then there's the computer geeks who fill their names into all the sign-in slots to just sit and game, leaving a rare fifteen-minute window for others to connect with the outside world. I nearly decked one of them one day, a scrawny little kid. His time was up and he was on the computer constantly. I went over and asked him to get off. He scoffed. I gave him two more minutes and then demanded he get off, pointing to the X on the screen to logout. The little punk slapped my hand away. He put his fucking hands on me! I fought the urge to hit him back and instead yelled for the security guard sitting not 10 feet away. He wouldn't do anything. I'm really not sure to this day what his job was. Nurses came. Nothing was done. Though I did get my computer back.

During one of my designated computer time slots, I tell Facebook I'm in the hospital. I don't really know why, I guess I need my friends, some sort of connection to the outside world. It's so lonely in here. There's no-touching rules and strict supervision through TVs. I feel like a trapped rat. I scratch my name "Riot" into a few walls, and sharpie "Riot on bitches" onto the stairs. I want to be remembered. I want to be heard. Maybe I'm just looking for attention. I don't get any.

Few of my friends know how to respond to my Facebook posts, and the outcry ends up making me feel more lonely. Now, looking back, I use my Facebook feed to try and piece together my adventures, finding it an interesting insight into my shifting mental state. Through it all I notice a common thread: the fight for good, a riot for the people.

I see my doctor every few days and she asks me questions like "do the birds still talk to you?" and "Are you still interested in finding Randy?" I am completely honest with her.

Soon I am let outside with Doctor Abbott. She brings me a cigarette. I thank her profusely. It feels lie years since I've had one. I delight in hearing the birds, though now they don't speak to me, but just chirp like they used to. I guess I should clarify a bit. The birds never spoke to me with voices, rather their actions said everything. They were like God incarnate, the Holy Spirit if you will, always watching from above. But today the birds are just birds. The air has never smelled so sweet though, fresh dewdrops slipping on the leaves. I kneel down and kiss the wet mossy ground before we head back, feeling like a prisoner in the jail shows I used to binge watch at home. It feels like forever since I've lived a normal life. I miss my couch, and my Netflix. I miss my family and my friends. Fuck, I miss my fucking dog! Thinking back to how easy it was to toss him out of the car, abandon him completely with a group of homeless strangers, my best friend for six years of my life...I know something was imbalanced in my brain. I've lost so many friends. I'm nearly 20 hours away from my family. It feels as though I've lost everything. The heavy automated doors swing open to people in wheelchairs with respirators and crutches and casts, holding books and scrolling phones while they wait.

I guess I'm in a hospital. And I guess I've got bipolar disorder. That's what they say anyway. I thought I was a healthy 28-year-old woman. I really don't know what to think anymore. It also hasn't really felt like a hospital. Even though the outside says St. Paul's, it feels more like something off of a reality show, something from the horror network. There's people drooling, pacing, laughing hysterically. It's nothing but designated pill times, and blood pressure checkers, needles, drawing of blood, doctors and nurses, every day a semi-controlled kind of chaos. One day a pill was dropped during medication time and three nurses spent nearly half an hour trying to find it. No pills go untaken or lost. Medications change on the daily. I used to ask what I was being given, but shit I don't know what any of this stuff is or what sorts of dosages are normal. All I can do is trust.

After a while I accumulate free time away from the ward, starting with two hours, then four, then the maximum of six. The smoker in me dies each morning, while I wait for my 2pm release time. Occasionally they have walks outside of the ward, of which I was permitted only one. They take a small group for a few block walk in Vancouver's downtown and then stop in at Tim Hortons for everyone to get something for under $3.00. I always wanted to buy two things that would cost less than 3 bucks but was not permitted. I cannot wait to be allowed out on my own!

Finally it's time, it's past 2pm, I've got my pass, and a friend asks me if I've been to the 4th floor. We walk through the empty hallways, up the elevator, past another wall of old nursing school photos, and out onto the veranda. It opens into a wide space lined with benches and gardening beds in the middle, blue skies above. Ignoring the signs, I scour the garden beds for sweet treats, finding a few baby tomatoes and some spinach leaves. We rarely get fresh food in the hospital, and I never steal more than a light snack. I call this place The Heavens and I visit here every day. I make a friend, an older Asian man who comes in his wheelchair, leg in a cast, and feeds the birds. Sometimes he shares a marijuana cigarette with me, and I think this man is like God. The birds seem to listen, and the birds always know. All animals do. They sense the energy of people, easily distinguishing good from bad intention. The more I think about it, the more I realize we all have this capacity, this kind of godliness. My journey affects your journey, in whatever slight way, we are all interconnected, it's that simple.

So, once I've acquired my pass, I spend my days entirely unsure of what to do with so much time. I had acquired the longest pass, six hours, and it felt necessary to spend all of it outside of the hospital's prison-like walls. Being a creature of habit, I develop a basic daily routine. First, a stop by the heavy-set Russian woman, who sits with her sons outside St. Paul's and sells cigarettes for $5.75 a pack. Next, on to the dispensary for a single joint. And last: the liquor store for a single beer, usually a tall can, something craft. Some days I just walk around while partaking in my daily treats, while others I'd pop up shop on Davies Street and enjoy the whir of the city around me. I dreamed of going to Granville Island or the art museum, but they all required a ferry or bus or some form of transportation that I was certain would get me back to the hospital past my curfew. I stayed within a ten-block radius at all times. I wanted nothing more than to be out of this prison, so I took my curfew and all the rules very seriously, even going so far as to buy my own watch. And even though I dreamed of catching a bus and living like a prisoner on the run, getting the fuck out of this place, I'm a good girl at heart...still, to this day.

This next collection of photos is a series of collages I made while in hospital. While out one day on one of my many 6 hour passes, I stumbled upon a large roll of discarded posterboard that had been coating a wall in Vancouver's downtown core. I carried the massive roll back to the ward and began ripping and snipping and then organizing the layers and pieces by colour in my tiny compartmentalized "bedroom", which was really two sheets separating me from the two other women in the room. I certainly looked like I belonged in the psych ward; papers flying, bits of colored shards all around me, and my passion palpable.

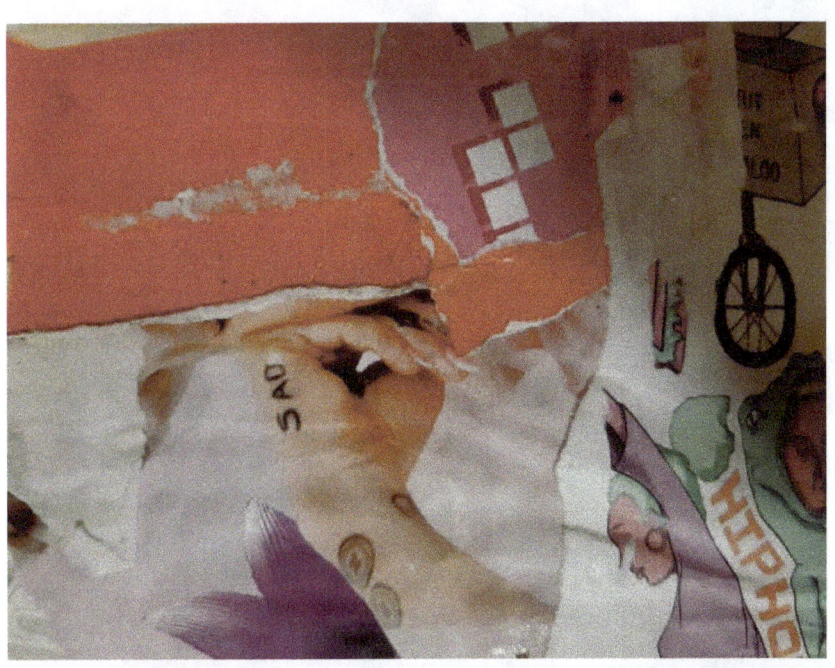

"Have I gone mad?

I'm afraid so, but let me tell you something, the best people usually are."

— Lewis Carroll, **Alice in Wonderland**

RIOT

END

RIOT

The day my parents came to visit me in the hospital was the most delicious thing I can remember in my life. The sweet nectar of their faces dripped in my memories for the next couple of weeks that I stayed in the ward. For a month and a half I'd been watching people's family members walk through the secured heavy metal doors, swinging open only to people on the list, like a high-end nightclub. And, as any arrival was cause to get up and see what was going on, they guarded those doors heavily. When my parents walked through they felt like a mirage, or a space age hologram. I didn't think it was real...until I fell into my mother's arms.

Of course James, the resident drama queen, had come over to see what was happening first, so I reluctantly introduced him and took my parents on a tour of the ward. I showed them the small room I shared with two other women, the TV room where I often fell asleep (even though we weren't allowed to), and the couple of quiet places where I would make my calls home to them. They had travelled nearly sixteen hours to get here, and the plan was to take my car back with them and I would fly home once released. Of course, the battery ended up being dead, that was five hundred dollars, and the tow bill over one thousand dollars. Plus, I'd been paying for my place in the Okanagan, spending cash each day, and making nothing...thank God my mom taught me to be a saver!

In the afternoon we travelled down to my *living room* at Broadway and Commercial to pin up posters I'd designed on the hospital's computer of my little lost Leo. It felt so strange to be back. Even though the sights and smells were the same, the sense of adventure was gone. I felt a flash of pride, however, showing my parents around the place I'd made my home for nearly a month. I pointed out every bit of graffiti I'd left, described the layout of the *rooms* in my parking lot *home*, and retraced numerous blurred memories. Then the day was dried up, and my parents had to leave. This was the least delicious feeling I've ever had in my life, having to wilfully leave my family and walk back into my prison.

Finally after another week, which felt like an eternity, I was able to be released. I packed up what few things I could fit into an ugly floral suitcase given to me by the hospital, gave the rest of my clothing back as a donation, left what snacks I had for the other patients, and with no room for my favourite blue robe (the one Theo had given me), I gifted it to

James, the fashionista. I left a little piece of Theo behind with that robe. With the entire experience really. Theo—the person I'd been most connected to for a third of my life—had no idea the shit I'd been going through and the tunnel I'd spiraled down. I like to think he would have cared had he known...but I have no way to tell. Initially he showed some concern, reaching out to my mother after hearing from friends that I wasn't acting myself. Most of them thought I was on drugs and just didn't know how to handle it. My roller derby team threatened to suspend me, many friends deleted me from their contacts, and I was fired from one of my favourite jobs. I remember being so incredibly angry at Theo for telling my mom, as if I were riding a wave of chaos and trying not to let her onto it until I surfed to the other side. He had betrayed me by going to the one person I was trying to hide everything from. Little did I know that the other side of the chaos wave was more like rock bottom.

I took a cab on the hospital's dime, rolling the windows as far down as they would go, forgetting how amazing the wind felt through my hair. I boarded the plane and departed without a hitch, and before I knew it I was driving home to Smithers with my dad. We stopped at Tim Hortons for a treat and I remember feeling so grateful for the pumpkin spice iced capp that I cried. I had my freedom back. I was allowed to spend more than three dollars. I could get whatever I wanted. We could stop again at the next one. I was free and well taken care of. My dad lit a cigarette and I giggled, remembering God under the bridge and how much he reminded me of him. And while likely just a man under a bridge, I remember being so thankful for the familiarity he brought back during a time of such discombobulation. I had missed my parents immensely.

I stay home recouping for the first month and some, allowing the medications to settle in my system. During that time I became visibly disabled. My hands shook, I couldn't smile or really move my face at all. I was restless during sleeping hours, only able to lay on the couch for 10 second increments before needing to pace the entire house for the night. I drooled. I was completely un-emotive. I looked and felt like a robot. It was dreadful.

One morning my shakes were especially bad and mom decided we should go to the emergency room. The doctor had me do a drawing test using each hand to draw a swirl, and a touch test, measuring my capacity to connect my fingertip with the doctor's. They discovered I had been overdosed on my medications before leaving St. Paul's Hospital. I just had to wait for the symptoms to wear off.

At some point my parents and I made the sixteen-hour journey to my funky suite in the Okanagan to pick up my stuff and say my goodbyes. It was a whirlwind three days. Since being in the hospital and posting flyers about my little lost Leo a woman named Angel had been in contact with me about finding my dog. After a couple of weeks of back and forth texting I was sure it was a sham and, as Dr. Abbott cautioned, maybe someone just trying to get money out of the deal. Once in the Okanagan, however, I got a picture. There he was. My scruffy little Leo, plain as day. So while mom stayed cleaning the suite, texting relentlessly with pictures of items from my home (the give, thrift, keep game) to par down the load, dad and I traveled another four hours to Vancouver, hoping Angel wouldn't flake this time. We got down to my *living room*, waiting for what seemed an eternity, and then with no patience left, seeing her far in the distance, I ran across the street to meet her and grab my puppy from her arms. She offered me a half can of wet dog food, a new leash, and some treats. I tried to offer her forty dollars, but she refused. She thought his owner may have died, considering where she'd picked him up. She said he was so sad, wandering the streets, looking lost and lonely. Now don't get me started on the irony of her name being Angel, I don't know how I feel about God and his master plan anymore, but I wasn't about to ask questions. I had my little man back, my little lost Leo. Everything was going to be ok.

The four of us travelled home to Smithers, and I lived in my parent's house for another eight months, sleeping on a mattress on their boot room floor. While not the most appealing solution, having moved out at seventeen and always being known as an independent young woman, I was surrounded by the love of my family and that was more than I could ask for. I woke every morning to smokes with my dad and fell asleep most nights on the couch watching a movie with him and mom. There was routine. It was nice.

But as with any routine, I grew tired of certain parts. Mom had searched around tirelessly online for a dresser. We were so far north, the closest selection of major department stores were four hours away in Prince George. So my life remained partially packed up in boxes in the shed, partially under the stairs, and the rest of it piled around the tiny boot room. Because of my weight gain, very little of my clothing fit anymore and I walked around in the same grubby hoodie and sweatpants, day after day. Sure, they were the ones God gave me, but they no longer made me feel powerful or sexy or any of the things I was looking to become again.

Once we were all comfortable with me driving, I would occasionally head the half hour into town to search for any clothes that fit at our two local thrift shops. It was so discouraging. I'd pull something off the rack I liked and it was always too small. Or I'd find three suitably sized dresses and they'd look terrible or completely go against the grain of my style. I was in a place of finding myself again. How was I to do it if I couldn't look like how I felt? I'd always worn funky bright colours and patterns, my inner artist loving to play through the garments I chose. But now I was faced with such little selection, it felt impossible.

Not only this, but while in the hospital I had decided to have all of my hair chopped off. At first I went at it with nail clippers, using the sharp edge to slice long strands away like they do when thinning your hair in a salon. I remember the one nurse was horrified, and kept saying that a volunteer hairdresser comes every couple of weeks and I should wait. I am not a patient human. So there I stood, next to the nurses station, staring down a girl I barely recognized in the mirror. She was in there somewhere. I knew it. If only I could trim her free. I sliced and shaved, making layers in my fine brown hair. It actually looked pretty good. But once break time came and I was free from the hospital for the day, I chose to find an alternative solution. I entered a barber shop, picked their coolest-looking mandala flower shave design, and let them get to work.

All my hair lay on the cool tiled floor, but I still didn't see Riot in the mirror...and the flower design looked like shit. Still I paid the guy and left into the busy Vancouver streets in search of myself.

Not only do my clothes not fit because, let's face it, I've gotten fat. But my head is buzzed and growing out like shit. I don't know who I see when I look in my parent's mirror, but I'm certain it's not myself. I try to practice smiling like I used to when I was a kid. "Such a gorgeous smile," Grandma would tell me, having a giggle as I practiced in her hallway mirror. I wanted to convey something with my smile. To make people feel welcomed and warm. I had always wanted that. And now, age 29, I was having to retrain my muscles to wear such honesty on my face again. But as my meds settled, this too became easier. I could move my face with more ease. The drooling stopped. I was finally able to sleep through the night.

There was hope.

Soon enough, I was looking at new places to live. And where else would I be pulled, but to the ocean. To my mother's disdain, I started looking at apartments in Victoria, a sixteen-hour drive away. It was somewhere I had always wanted to live. Since I was eighteen and university shopping, Victoria had always been a dream destination. At the time it was just too expensive to be feasible...and it seems that that's still the case. Bedrooms in someone's house are going for eight to nine hundred dollars. Mom thought it was too far away. What if I went manic again? Who would help me? Up north in Smithers, where my parents lived, I had a doctor. I had a medication plan that was just starting to feel balanced.

I now had a job (albeit at Canadian Tire, but I had a source of income). My life was just beginning to settle again. Why would I upset all that?

Still, something in me longed for the ocean and the independence. And then I found it! An apartment in downtown Victoria: the Chelsea Apartments! Now I'll let you in on a little secret, Riot may be my nickname, but Chelsea is the name my mother gave me at birth...so this apartment seemed meant to be. I called them and arranged an appointment, setting off in my tiny red Caviar Can once again in search of an adventure. I can't say exactly how my mother must have felt, but I'm sure it was a compilation of nervousness, fear, and hope maybe.

I met with the apartment manager, and only that one. I was sure it was meant to be. I had also printed out resumes that I scattered around the neighborhood surrounding the Chelsea Apartments. While I didn't hear God calling to me in the same way anymore, I knew that it all was going to align according to His plan.

Unfortunately however, the apartment was on the sixth floor, nestled in a not so nice part of town, and there was a waitlist. I also didn't have any source of income on the island and my parents wouldn't co-sign for me. I remember being so frustrated with them. For the first time in my life they didn't believe I could do it. Not only that, but they didn't believe I *should* do it. Once again I felt oppressed by somebody else's concerns or agenda. With Theo we had virtually always moved for his work. And now, a single, somewhat healthy young woman, I wanted to make that decision based solely on myself. I didn't want to listen to my parents. I just wanted to do what I wanted to do. I mean, wasn't that my right?

I returned to Smithers quite discouraged. I knew the Chelsea Apartments weren't meant for Chelsea. And I knew my parent's boot room wasn't for me either. The more my mother spoke, the more it all seemed to make sense. I could start small and move somewhere nearby: into the heart of Smithers, maybe Terrace, Prince Rupert if I wanted to be near the ocean. I could stay until my meds were settled, in the safety net of family nearby—a luxury I hadn't had in the past ten years living with Theo. I could find a job in retail or waitressing again, and start there to find my happiness.

I took it to heart, and soon enough found a sweet little suite right in Smithers. A fifteen-minute walk to my mom's work, a way shorter drive to my new friends, and a lovely trail for Leo and I a couple blocks away. I knew it wasn't everything I was looking for, but I knew it was good.

I stayed there a full year, as my sister suggested. "Takes a full year of seasons to really know a place." I'd started to really settle into a life I enjoyed. I worked nights at a local pub, made friends with some of the girls. We'd go out dancing at the only bar in town—only on Saturdays, of course, too sleazy any other night. I put out feelers into my roller derby community and found a team in Terrace that I'd travel six hours to practice with. It felt so good to be back on my skates! I went for walks with Leo, floated the river, and tried to embrace the slowness of northern living. Soon enough, I'd helped start a team all our own called the Bulkley Valley Bruisers who practiced in Smithers and Houston. Slowly, but surely, badass northern women heard the callout and joined our league. It felt so good to be surrounded by personalities I emulated: strong beautiful women in all shapes and sizes coming together to kick ass.

Now I get injections every month and take pills every day and I feel more and more like myself all the time. Sure, I have my issues with Big Pharma running my body, but I've seen the alternative. I've seen the depression side and the manic side of being bipolar. I know I like a steady level; the level I grew up with for 26 years of my life before being blindsided. They say I can go off meds after two years, which brings us to right about now, but honestly this scares me also. Would I feel a swing coming on? Would I know how to seek help? Or would I find that chaos wave and get taken even further, even deeper, loving its tumultuous eb and flow? I don't even trust myself to know anymore.

Sep. 22, 2018

 Fine Balance Yoga
Sep. 15, 2018

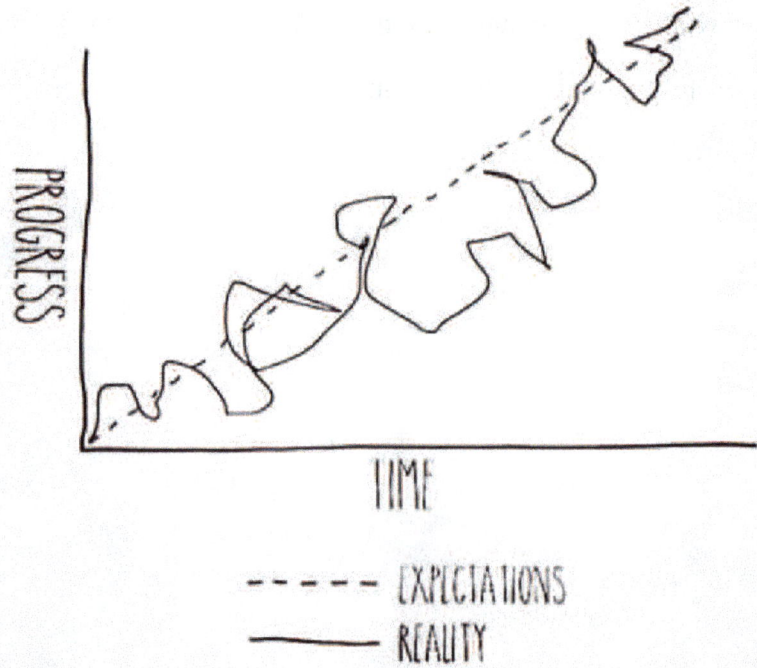

RIOT

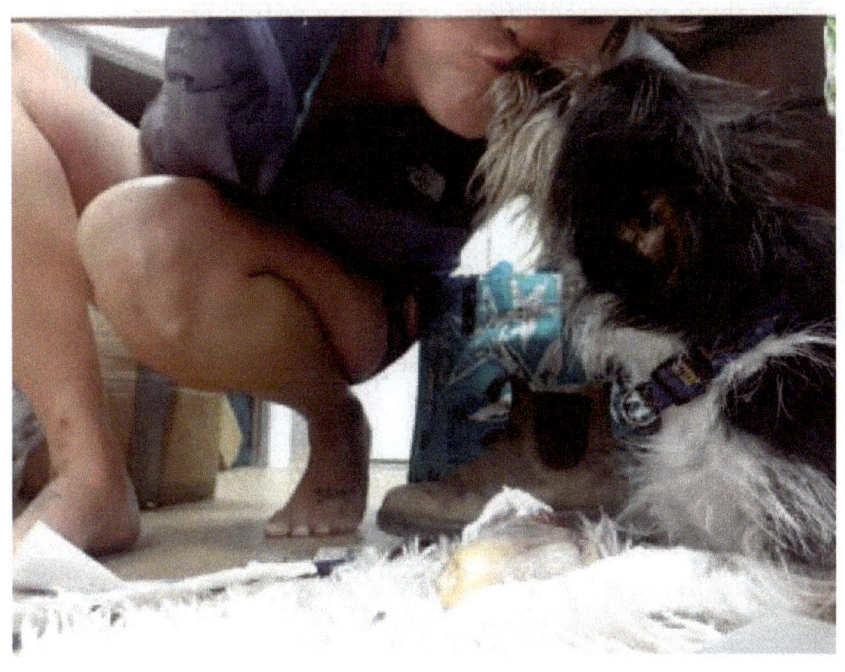

"Taking responsibility is kind of a painful experience. I had to make peace with this manic version of myself and sit down and think well when I'm manic, that's also when I make my best art, It's when I'm the most compassionate. It's the version of me that's given me everything that I have."

-Halsey

NEW BEGINNING

I open the shiny red door of my Caviar Can and am confronted with an immovable wall of stuff. One more load of clothing (wrapped precariously in a blue Canadian Tire tarp) to cram into some cranny somewhere and I'm set—it's all packed up. My life that is. Everything essential I own, and my tiny little dog, packed into my Honda Fit and ready for the next great adventure—my new beginning.

I grab gas down the block, check the tires, and hit the open road. It's early, but I still plan to pop in for a coffee with mom and dad.

We hug lots. Drink two cups instead of one. Dad asks if I've checked the tires. Mom kisses my forehead. And I'm off.

Riot onward!

About a month ago I found an ad on Kijiji for a suite in Victoria. I hadn't planned to move until the spring, once the snow had cleared, but this place was in my budget. It allowed pets. And there was no question of income. Plus the snow hadn't started to fly yet, so I could get down there with ease. All I had to do was deposit five hundred dollars.

I thought it might be a scam.

But hell, I know I'm not happy up north. My family's here, but something's missing. I need my spark back, and there's something about the big city I think might help. If I show up and the house doesn't exist, I'll find a motel room. I've got the cash again. I feel a bit of worry, but mostly elation. I'm finally going to live where I've always wanted to. I'm going to start fresh, do exactly what I want, when I want. And I've got no one but myself and my dog to consider.

I finish out the last week of shifts at the pub, and in that time receive the biggest tip I've ever seen in my career. Would you believe it, 500$? I take it as a sign and set it aside for my new house, my new life, my new beginning.

Two days and sixteen hours of driving later I pull into the cute little driveway that fits my cute little Caviar Can perfectly. Here I meet Allan, my new landlord. He seems nice. He's even furnished the tiny suite for me with everything I would need, which is perfect because I don't own a bed or a dresser or a table. I have a box of homemade dishes, my clothes, and a stack of cash-out papers from work I recycled to start writing this book. I make sure I also bring a chair for sitting outside as I expect it will be one of my favorite writing and smoking spots. Allan has papers to sign and inspections to do and then it's all mine, my own little home on the island.

I spend my first days organizing and meeting the other women who live in the house. Three suites, three single women, all with dogs. It's kind of perfect.

I then make a list of what I'd like to accomplish on the island.

My list came out like this:

1. Find a pottery studio
2. Sign up for roller derby
3. Write this book
4. Go to the beach
5. Visit new restaurants
6. Road trip
7. Go camping
8. Get a job

As getting a job is nowhere near the top of my list, I end up spending four months blissfully living off savings, making pottery all day and writing late into the night at my favourite diner, Denny's. It's here that I meet my new best friend, Gwen. She's got wild curly hair and always wears a smile on her face, no matter how shitty the customers. I see her here most nights. She never seems annoyed that I sit for hours on my laptop sipping refillable coffees. One night, I sat for probably fourteen hours, really making progress on the writing. She comes around to tell me she'll be going off shift. Hell, it's already 4am! I ask what she's gonna do after shift and she says she's going home to drink a bottle of wine. I laugh and ask if she wants company. This was the moment our friendship was born.

Gwen and I go adventuring almost every day. She's indecisive and also new to the island, so I usually pick what we'll do. This is so new to me. Not only do I do the driving, but I plan the adventures. It feels liberating. We visit beaches, try out new restaurants, drive by parliament at night just to see the lights and then drink bubbly at the wharf and watch the boats late into the evening. This becomes our place: fisherman's wharf. It feels good to have a friend, an adventure buddy, and obviously Mr. Leo (our Little Man) always accompanies.

When I'm not hanging out with Gwen, I sleep in, visit art museums, go on dates. I meet a friend for espresso martinis at the waterfront. I brunch downtown. I live my life just as I want to live it. And as before I feel an excitement and lightness in my spirit that's unprecedented by any typical pathway to success.

Then the time comes that I need to make money, and suddenly the bars are closing down. I can't find waitressing work anywhere. A virus has come from Asia, and suddenly the whole world is wearing masks, dousing their hands in sanitizer, and buying up all the toilet paper. It goes from zero to sixty in a few days, and I know I've got to change my game plan.

So one day I'm driving to Walmart to get groceries and decide to bypass the pandemonium of such a large store and pop into a smaller, more local grocer. I tour around a bit, enjoying the luxuries that come with a nicer grocery store: non-fluorescent lighting, locally grown produce, and a nice big deli. Seeing this, I have a thought. I leave my cart and run out to the car for a resume. "You were so ballsy," some of my coworkers told me later, having walked up and requested the deli manager personally. I don't remember being ballsy as much as desperate for a paycheque. I had a quick chat with the deli manager, and then the store's manager, and a few days later I was hired.

Having worked in a deli back in Penticton, I was already equipped to be successful and I knew I enjoyed the work. I spend my days preparing all sorts of meals and snacks, cooking for the public, and slicing meat. I was shocked how quickly and easily everything came back to me, and even though the paycheque sucks, I can confidently pay rent, which is what really matters.

Some days I still have reservations about the choices I've made. Six-and-a-half years of university and here I am making sandwiches like I was sixteen again. I know I can do better, be better, give something back to my community. But I am learning that doesn't always have to be one's career. I don't go home and worry about the fact that I sliced too much honey ham, or forgot the soya sauce packet with the noodles. I clock out and I'm out. If I were teaching, I would have to stay marking and prepping for hours. I would go home and prep even more late into the night and then wake hours before school to second guess and rehash my lesson plans for the day. I would get paid for eight hours, work sixteen, and never turn my brain off from school. I would worry about the kids, wonder if they've had breakfast, try to mitigate disasters all day long, just to do it all over again. I would be exhausted and likely part of the fifty percent of teachers that quit in the first five years (a fact I was told in my first teaching session!). Is a career really worth my life?

Through my transition I've learned that I am selfish with my time and energy. I'm not willing to give my everything for someone else's kids. And even though that means a smaller paycheque, it allows me my life back. I am here to make a difference. I know that. So today I do it through my smile and good nature. I try to pass this smile onto my coworkers and the public I serve. I tell jokes and start deep conversations. I try to make work not so much like work. Hell, we have to be here eight hours a day, why not have some fun while doing it?

I'm also trying to make a difference with this story.

Of course I still struggle with my sense of purpose for my life. And I feel like one day I'll find a career that is more suitable. But for now, this is good. I'm living where I've always wanted to live, I'm paying for the roof over my head and the fancy cheese I love for my stomach. My dog and my new budgies, fish, and frogs are well cared for. I've got friends here now, and am following my passions. I'm not completely certain what success looks like, but I think I'm almost there.

The next step is finishing this book.

And then *shudder* sharing it with the world.

I've thought a lot about this. I'm most nervous to share this story with Theo. It's been a couple years since we broke up and I so desperately want him to know what I went through, what I *was* going through, and how little I could trust my own sense of rationality. I was not myself. I was a cruel and irrational version of me. For years I was not the self I had grown to love. I was someone different. Someone distant. Someone lost. And someone clinging to someone else in hopes of finding that someone again.

It wasn't fair.

I should have left long before I did. I needed change. Apparently I needed to snap to resettle; almost like faults in the earth's tectonic plates, something needed to shift to relieve the pressure building inside me.

Looking back, this book actually feels a bit like a love letter...both to Theo and to the general masses. Sure, it started as my own cathartic approach at remembering just what the hell I'd gone through. But it's morphed into so much more than that. It's a love letter to humanity. It pleads for people's empathy. I hope that translating my pain into these pages will leave you questioning your predispositions not only about other people, but perhaps about yourself. As a species, we need more humility. We always forget how fragile we truly are.

I sit in my gated patio facing the busy McKenzie Ave, letting the hum of ongoing traffic lull my stories into text. My gently frosted twinkle lights set an ambiance for the writing I do late into the evening, almost every evening as of late. I need this book completed this year. It's become my new mission. I want to write a book by age thirty. How cool would that be? I mean, what is the point of going through so much if not to share and help alleviate others? I'm not one to bottle in pain. I'd rather release it, analyze it, and learn and grow from it. Of course I am nervous to share my story. As you've found out, it's very personal and convoluted. I didn't always do the right thing, I'm not always lit in the best light. I didn't get here on a straight path. But how boring would it be if I had?

Are there things I would change about my journey? Of course! I would have scoped out clinical help long before exhausting Theo and losing the love of my life. I would have listened to my intuition sooner and spoke about the things I kept secret in my journal. I wouldn't have suffered alone for so long.

And it's my greatest hope that by sharing my story you may not have to suffer alone either.

Mental illness can happen to anyone, even those who seem the most put together. Sometimes we're hiding tears behind a smile. Other times it looks like the fetal position over a bottle of wine because we don't know where else to turn. That bottle of wine sometimes turns to several.

Anything for an escape. Sometimes the wine turns to drugs. The drugs turn to divorce, lost jobs, broken families, and homelessness. Sometimes the people around you just aren't equipped to carry the baggage you've learned to carry on your own.

This is why I beg you not to keep everything hidden in the covers of a journal or buried deep inside like I did for so many years. People love you. People care about your well being. They may not all be certified to help, but there are psychiatrists and counsellors who are. It's never too late to speak up, to ask for help, or to reach out to a person in crisis.

Sometimes people make comments about how far I've come or about avoiding becoming *that person* again. I want to make it clear: I have always lived with this disorder, it had just not manifested itself clearly before. I am not a different person than I was when manic. It's not a Jekyll and Hyde situation. It's two sides of the same coin. I can't discredit who I was or what I did because it brought me here. I learned so much, not only about myself, but about life, and working hard and persevering. I learned that life can turn you sideways in minutes, take you places you never thought you'd be: sleeping under bridges, living in your car, maybe spending a night or two in jail. I learned that we really aren't in control of our destinies, as much as people cling to that hope.

To be honest, I don't know exactly what I believe anymore when it comes to deities. I like to think we are all God, each being breathing life into another. I find myself pondering seemingly absurd things like: do the trees get depressed? Can an ant go manic? Just because we can identify a disorder, is it our right to alter it? People are no longer called disabled, but differently abled. Why can't we be differently minded and accepted as such? Were the oracles of ancient Roman times speaking to God because of a mental disorder or did we just accept it as being in an enlightened state, something to be revered even?

I don't have a resolute answer to any of these questions, and all I can draw from is my own story. All I know is that I am incredibly thankful for the medications, doctors, social workers, family, friends, and random strangers that helped get me through. In any other circumstance I could still be living on the streets in East Vancouver, likely drug addicted and lost.

RIOT

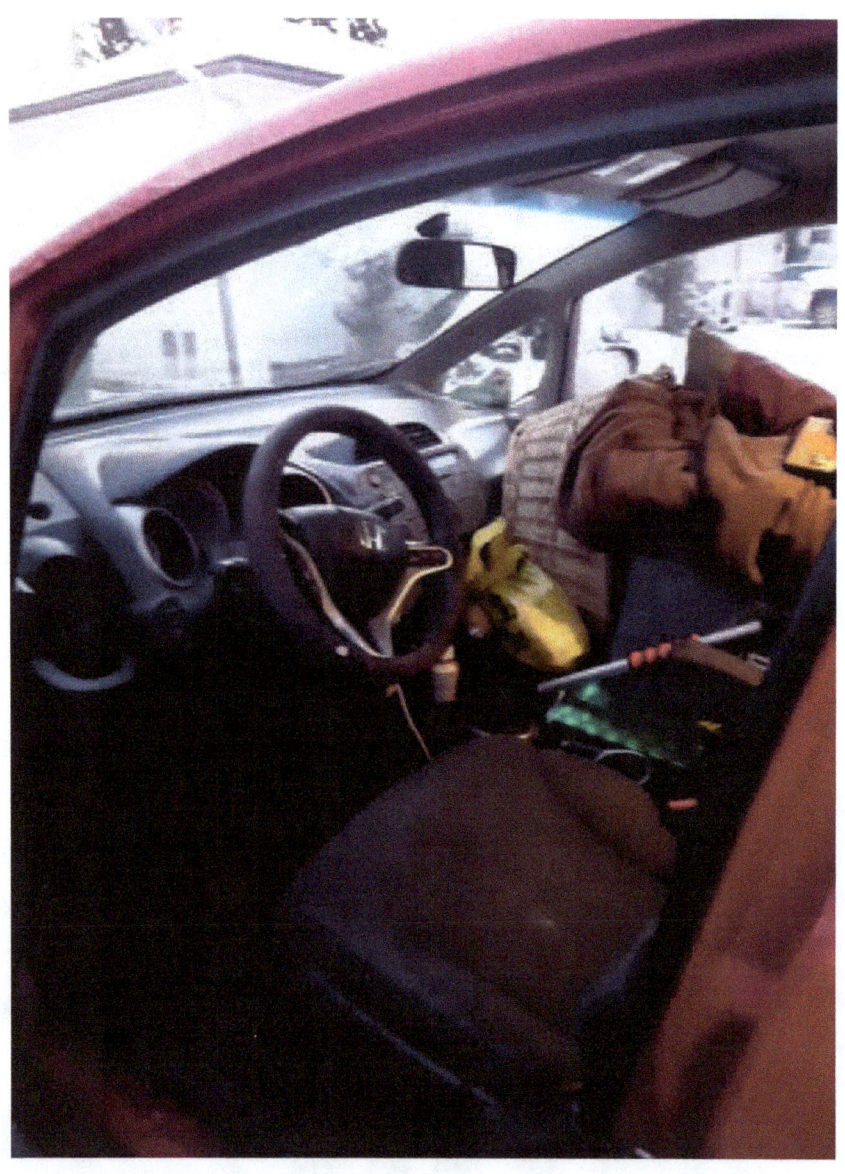

You should dance with the skeletons in your closet.
Learn their names,
so you can ask them to leave.
Have coffee with your demons.
Ask them important questions like, "What keeps you here?"
Learn what doors they keep finding open, and kick them out.

Final Thanks

My final thanks goes out to the unknown lawyer who pled my case while I was in the psych ward. Unbeknownst to me, I had been added to an online registry of people who have criminal charges in Canada. And Theo's family, being tied in with the police force professionally, somehow caught wind of my charges. In a one-off spontaneous phone call to Theo, when visiting the Okanagan two summers after everything unfolded, I discovered he knew more about my trials than I had ever imagined. The phone call did not go well, though he didn't hang up immediately as I had suspected he would. Instead, he listened to me for a brief minute or two before throwing accusations of these charges in my face. I was immediately bewildered, again having no idea myself that I had acquired such a record. I played it off however, pretending I'd known all along. Immediately after he told me to "fuck off" and we hung up semi-peaceably - all things considered - with a "goodbye" on each end, I called my mother.

"Was I criminally charged?"

"Yes you were."

End of story.

I knew she'd made numerous phone calls for me, with neither the police nor hospital able to confirm my whereabouts or well being due to confidentiality restrictions. She called transition houses and various jails, the hospital, and even filed a missing person's report. I knew she'd been tireless in her efforts, as she did eventually find me. But I had no idea she'd pled for my charges to be wiped.

Apparently she'd told someone along the line a bit about my history and that I'd been going to school to be a teacher. As I wouldn't be able to practice teaching with a criminal record, that someone told someone else in the courthouse, and someone else took it upon themselves to stand up for me in court when I couldn't stand up for myself. I am beyond grateful for your kindness, whoever you are. God or no God, you are most certainly an angel in my story. Thank you.

And lastly, I want to thank YOU again, from the bottom of my heart, for taking your precious time to read my stories and interact with some of the most influential characters in my tale thus far. I would also like to invite you to share your own mental health stories (big or small, seemingly influential or meaningless) at "Shed the Shame" on Facebook, in hopes of empowering others to shed the shame.

Mental illness is a topic we will eventually all have to deal with, whether on our own journey or in our connections with others. The mind, being such a complex and beautiful place—while also fragile and fluid—should be revered, respected, and its well being never taken for granted. We are blessed each day to live our lives, my journey affecting your journey. We are all one world. And thus our stories unfold, united at their core, but oh so drastically different at the same time

Be kind humans.

yes,
not everything went
as planned. in fact
it all fell apart.

terribly.
spectacularly.

no problem.
the pieces are all
still there. i can
put them back together
in a new way.

that's the power
of hope.

/ topher kearby

You are not
the darkness
you endured.

You are the
light that
refused to
surrender.

John Mark Green

National Suicide Prevention Lifeline: 1 800 273 8255

Crisis Services Canada: 1 833 456 4566

1 800 SUICIDE: 1 800 784 2433

Mental Health Support: 310 6789 (no area code needed)

Kid's Help Phone: 1 800 668 6868

Youth in BC.com: 1 604 872 3311

Alcohol and Drug Information and Referral Service: 1 800 663 1441

"Everyone you meet is fighting

a battle you know nothing about.

Be kind.

Always."

-Robin Williams

www.ingramcontent.com/pod-product-compliance
Lightning Source LLC
Chambersburg PA
CBHW051527020426
42333CB00016B/1813